AN APPROACH TO TYPE

With 26 soldiers of lead I will conquer the world !

JOHN R. BIGGS MSIA ATD

AN APPROACH TO

BLANDFORD PRESS LONDON: MCMLXI

First published in 1949. Second Edition 1961
by the Blandford Press, West Central Street, W.C.1.
Printed by Tonbridge Printers Ltd., Peach Hall Works,
Tonbridge, Kent, on paper supplied by Alex. Cowan &
Sons Ltd. with Ultraset Antique Black ink supplied by
Richardson Printing Ink Co. Ltd.

Contents

The woodengravings on pages 8, 50, 53, 54, 136 are from J. & R. M. Wood's Typographic Advertiser, 1864. They were stock blocks sold to printers who could insert their own words in place of those shown.

Preface

THIS book grew out of repeated suggestions by students at the London School of Printing and the Central School of Arts & Crafts that talks I gave there should be made available in print. It does not claim to be more than the talks were originally intended for, namely, introductory remarks to a study of type faces. Many students wanted aids to the recognition of type faces, and few at the outset could distinguish between 'old face' and 'modern'. Type specimens were unobtainable except when a student managed to acquire an old printer's specimen book, which was rarely much use because of the large number of bad types usually included. Students could not be expected to discriminate between the good and the bad, in fact, all too often students were attracted by the eccentricities of the bad types. Some specimen books print the same phrase over and over again so that certain letters of the alphabet are absent throughout the book. A student who hopes to take up layout must practise lettering, and for this purpose complete alphabets in large sizes are included as examples from which to copy.

There have been a number of books on the market which gave complete alphabets in a large size, but a student of layout needs more than a specimen to copy. He wants to know what other sizes are at his disposal. He needs to know whether italic is included in every size and which sizes have small caps in the fount. A need was felt for a specimen book which gave a complete fount with caps, lower-case, figures and italic in the largest size, followed by a small quantity of each other size.

An attempt is made here to meet such a need. As all the types in this book can be obtained through Trade Typesetters the student typographer can be sure that these types can be bought without very much trouble. How many young designers have specified a type for a job only to be told that it is unobtainable! Practical printers will appreciate the importance of studying types which can be procured without a lot of correspondence and long delays.

Nevertheless, there is a wide variety of types available on the Linotype and Intertype (two independent companies producing slug-setting machines); on the Ludlow (a slug-setting machine where the matrices are set by hand); and on the Monotype. There is also a large number of interesting and useful types for hand-setting which can be obtained from the various typefounders of Britain, America and the Continent of Europe.

The number of type faces displayed in this book is comparatively small because I firmly believe that it is not a good thing for a beginner to concern himself with many designs; far better to concentrate on a few reputable faces. But once a reasonable amount of skill and judgment has been acquired the student can enjoy himself experimenting with whatever takes his fancy, whether it be classic roman, script, or the fantastic forms that come and go in advertisements.

At the same time it may be doubted whether there is really any need for the large number of different type designs which exist. Edward Johnston when asked to design a good book type replied with characteristic drollery: 'There is one already'.

No apology is required for the short history of the alphabet, which I hope will lead to more students following up the study in the books recommended in the bibliography. Updike in his great work *Printing Types* says: 'So it is clear that we can have no knowledge of the types of today and their history without knowing the history of types back to the invention of printing, and that we can have no knowledge of the first types or their relative place in the scheme of things, unless we know how earlier calligraphers formed the letters of their manuscript book-hands. Nor can we tell how the letter-forms themselves came to be unless we know the history of the alphabet'.

Thanks are due to Sir Francis Meynell and Ellis Thirkettle for inspiration and criticism, and to the following for permission to use type specimens, photographs, or for help in other ways. Messrs. Stephenson, Blake & Co. Ltd., The Monotype Corporation, Messrs. Harrap, Linotype & Machinery Ltd., Douglas Cleverdon, Messrs. Longmans Green & Co., Berthold Wolpe, Messrs. Sir Isaac Pitman & Sons, Ltd., The Bowater Paper Corporation Ltd.

What is Type?

THE word type can be used in many senses, but for the purpose of this book two senses only need to be defined. In typography a type may mean the shape or image as it appears on paper—a thing of two dimensions having only length and breadth; or it may mean the actual type made of metal—a thing of three dimensions having length, breadth and height. The designer, typographer, layout-man, call him what you will, deals mainly with the shapes as they appear on paper, but in order fully to appreciate those forms a knowledge and understanding of the underlying processes is necessary.

In order to overcome the ambiguity of the word type, printers often use the word 'sort' when referring to the metal type or 'stamp'. It is usually used in the sense of individual letters; thus when the compositor runs out of some letters and cannot continue with his work he says he is 'out of sorts'. He may then order from the type-founder a quantity of extra letters at 'sorts rate' which is more expensive than when buying a large quantity. The diagram opposite shows what the metal printing type looks like. Most of the terms require no explanation, but the word 'beard' needs amplification. The part referred to in this diagram as the beard, one famous authority describes as the 'shoulder'; and the part here called the 'bevel' (which it obviously is) he describes as 'beard or neck'. After making a careful check on general usage of the word beard, there seems little doubt that the average printer or compositor today when he talks about the beard, means the space below the base-line.

Enclosed shapes such as are found in lower-case e and a are called counters. That word carries us back to the days when all the processes of making type were carried out by hand. The matrix from which the letter was cast was not engraved direct, but was made with a punch the same shape as the letter. This was made not only with gravers, but mainly with files and other abrasives so that great refinement of shape was possible. Difficulty arose with the tiny enclosed shapes and it was found best to make another punch which was driven into the master-punch. This would, in its turn, be driven into another piece of metal to form the matrix. The word 'counter-punch' was used to distinguish it from the master-punch; hence the shapes made by the counter-punch are called counters. In the smaller sizes of type the counters are made proportionately larger than in the bigger sizes otherwise they would fill in with ink too quickly.

Matrixes are still struck from punches today but the punches are rarely cut by hand, and it is to be feared that the skilled manual punch-cutter is almost extinct.

A new type generally begins with a drawing on paper of a size convenient to the artist,

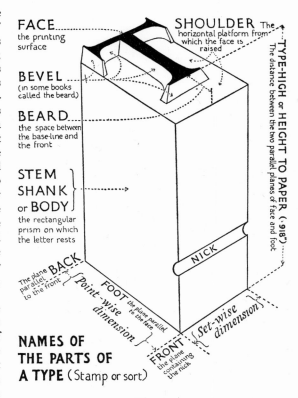

Fig. 1.

often about 2 in. high. The ideal is for the drawing to be the actual size of the type intended, but for the smaller sizes this becomes impractical for most people, indeed, many skilled letters find it an ordeal to make letters less than half an inch high. When the punches were cut by hand and modifications of proportion necessary in each size were generally made by the craftsman because he actually worked the same size as the finished letter. Today it is possible for a man to design or play an influential part in the design of a type, who has never handled a graver or a file. A type must begin with a carefully thought out drawing at such a size as the artist finds necessary to make his subtleties clear to other craftsmen. This letter is then projected by a kind of magic lantern on to a screen so that the image is about 10 in. high. It is then carefully traced on a sheet of paper. Highly skilled draughtsmen then go over this drawing making it sharp and precise, as it will form the master pattern for a relief model about 3 inches high. A pantographic machine is used that cuts through a layer of wax on a sheet of glass, making an exact reduced copy of the original which is being traced by the operator. An outline only is cut through the wax at this stage. The wax is then removed from inside the letter and an electrotype made which constitutes the perfect pattern from which the punch is cut. Note that this master pattern is a letter standing in relief.

The manufacture of the punch involves another important invention—the Pierpont punch-cutting machine which works to the accuracy of one twenty-five-thousandth part of an inch. It involves a pantograph, one end of which has a pointer which the operator traces round the master relief pattern just described. The other end carries a small cutting tool revolving at a high speed which cuts in steel a reduced replica of the pattern being traced by the operator. The final shape of the letter depends very largely on the accuracy of this machine, and the punches, after they have been cut, are examined microscopically so that a punch as near perfect as is technically possible is produced. The steel is hardened to withstand the strain of being struck into a piece of copper alloy which will be the matrix. Great accuracy is necessary to make sure that the letter is struck in the right place on the matrix-blank in order that capitals and lower-case align with one another. The copper alloy matrix may then be chromium plated in order to withstand the wear

and tear and the high temperature of the casting machine.

In the casting machine the matrix is carefully placed in the right position over the mould of the body. There is generally a little space on either side of the letter as well as at the foot so that the printing surface is not vertically above the body. This space, though minute in itself, affects the look of a page of type very considerably as all letters should appear to be evenly spaced and avoid the unpleasant bunching of certain letter sequences. When the matrix is in the correct relation to the mould of the body, type metal is then pumped in and the letter cast. It is then trimmed at the foot to the correct height (the height of a shilling on its edge), or more accurately 0.918 inches.

The nick which is to be seen on the front of the body is a guide to the compositor so that he can tell at a glance whether all the sorts in his stick are the right way round. Foundry type as distinct from 'MONOTYPE', may have two or three nicks in different positions on the body so that italic or small caps may be readily distinguished.

The Point System

PRINTERS do not measure their types or printing materials in inches or centimetres but in a special typographical point which only relates in an irregular manner to either the English or the Metric system of measurement. This is to be regretted but accepted, as nothing short of an atomic catastrophe is likely to bring about a reform of a system so widely used.

There are roughly 72 points to an inch (more precisely 0.9962 in.) and this unit of 1/72 in. is used in multiples to measure all typographic material. Twelve points, still often referred to by the old name of pica, is a unit used for measuring the lengths of lines of type. The length of a line of type is called the 'measure'. Hence the measure of a line would be given (unless otherwise stated) in multiples of 12 pt. (pica). Apart from the word 'pica,' the only other old name which survives in general use is 'nonpareil' for 6 pt. The older generation of compositors still use many more of the old names, but the young apprentice has to learn most of them from books rather than in the workshop.

A point system was developed in France in the eighteenth century—the French were ever a logical race—but it was not until 1886 that the American typefounders nominated a committee to consider the point system, and in 1898 the point sytem was adopted in England. Even today a few of the old, odd sizes may be found in long-established printing houses.

Until the adoption of a point system, types had borne no mathematical relationship to one another nor did the sizes of one typefounder agree precisely with the sizes of another. It was thus impossible to mix the type from two different founders. Sizes were given names, some of them reasonable, some of them charming. Who cannot enjoy such names as Agate, Ruby, Diamond, Brevier, Canon, Great Primer and Nonpareil? though this latter is commonly pronounced as 'nonprull'. Delightful though these names are, the logic and reasonableness of the point system commends itself, and only a sentimentalist would regret the change from irregular sizes with romantic names to prosaic numbers with the satisfaction of accurate and orderly progressing sizes.

Another term which must be introduced is the 'em'. Strictly, an em is the square of any body size, and there is such a square sort cast in every size for spacing purposes. It is thus correct to refer to a 6 pt. em, a 10 pt. em, a 72 pt. em. The tyro is often perplexed after learning this to hear a printer say, 'The measure of such-and-such a job is so many ems'. He would be justified in asking, 'What size of em?' if he did not know that it is the custom of the printing trade to mean 12 pt. (pica) ems unless another size is stated. On such an occasion the printer would say 'So many 8 pt. ems', or whatever point size is intended.

The pica or 12 pts., then, is approximately one-sixth of an inch, and for measures of only a few inches the beginner can safely work on that assumption. But as 12 points are really slightly less than 1/6 in. 72 picas falls short of a foot by about 1/16 in. This ambiguous use of the word em has only custom to support it, and many of the more thoughtful members of the craft argue for the retention of the word pica as the unit of measurement. Some already consistently specify measures in picas.

Half an em is known as an 'en', the set width of which is half the body size, i.e., a 12 pt. en will be 12 pts. × 6 pts. Like ems, ens are cast as spaces in every size of type. Owing to the resemblance of the sounds em and en, they might easily be misunderstood, and in order to avoid this possibility printers among themselves will describe an em as a 'mutton' and speak lightly of an en as a 'nut'. For example, the compositor might say that he intends to put a mutton space after a full-point, while a thoughtful typographer might reply that he would prefer a nut. In this instance the typographer would not be expressing a desire for a luxury food but for a nut space after every full-point.

In every size of type there are other standard widths of spaces besides ems (muttons) and ens (nuts). All these spaces have the same point dimension (see diagram on page 7) as every other sort, and in appearance each is a rectangular prism (the body) like a type, but without a letter rising from the platform known as the shoulder. Being below type height these spaces hold the printing sorts apart without themselves making any impression on the paper.

Nut and mutton spaces are also known as quads, or strictly, quadrats. Quadrats are also made in 2, 3 and 4 em lengths. These are used to fill out the lines at the end of paragraphs, the space on either side of a short headline or other similar occasions.

Below, spaces are raised to the same height as type so that they print as a square or rectangle and give a clear idea of the relative size of these spaces in 12 pt.

- em quadrat (mutton), the square of the body.
- en quad (nut), 1/2 body or two to the em.
- thick space, 1/3 body or three to the em.
- middle space, 1/4 body or four to the em.
- thin space, 1/5 body or five to the em.
- hair space, 1/12 body approx. A few exceptions are given below.

Fig. 2. Spaces.

Where one-twelfth of the body does not result in a thickness which relates conveniently to the point system it is made to the nearest half point. For example, in 6 pt. the hair space is 1/2 pt. In 12 pt. it is 1½ pts., in 18 pt. it is two points, and in 24 pt. the hair space is 3 pts.

In addition, hair spaces can be obtained in brass, one point (1/72 in.) in thickness, and in copper, which is but half a point thick (1/144 in.). Hair spaces are invaluable to the typographer who wishes to see his lines of caps evenly spaced.

The spacing material described so far is that employed to space words or letters horizontally, and which has the pointwise dimension the same as that of the type with which it is used. Letters having been correctly spaced as words and lines then need spacing into well-proportioned pages. This is achieved by means of strips of metal or wood of varying thicknesses that are placed between the lines. The thinnest strips of metal used for this purpose are known as leads (pronounced 'leds') and are 1, 1½, 2 and 3 pts. in thickness. The 1½ pt. leads are called thin, and the 3 pt. are referred to as thick. Thus when a typographer says a page of type requires thin

leading he means that 1½ pt. leads should be placed between each line. (Below, leads are brought up to type high so that they print and give a clear idea of their thickness.)

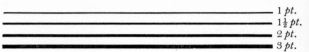

1 pt.
1½ pt.
2 pt.
3 pt.

Thicker strips, from 6 to 18 pt. are described as clumps and may be of either wood or metal. Spacing material of greater dimensions is known as furniture. Leads, clumps and furniture are cut to any required length, but generally to the following useful measures: 4, 5, 6, 7, 8, 9, 10, 12, 14, 15, 16, 18, 20, 22, 24, 25, 30, 35, 40 and 45 ems.

There is yet another kind of spacing material, rectangular prisms of type-metal, hollowed out to save metal, and known as quotations. These are normally made in the following sizes, the length and breadth being given in 12 pt. ems: 2 × 3, 4, 5, 6; 3 × 3, 4, 5, 6; 4 × 4, 5, 6; 5 × 5; 6 × 6, 9.

Quotations are used to fill in the large spaces in a title-page, at the head of chapters, surrounding blocks, etc.

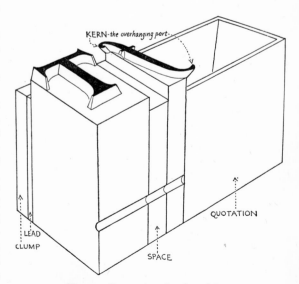

KERN-*the overhanging part*
QUOTATION
LEAD
CLUMP
SPACE

Fig. 3. Quotation, lead and kern.

It may not be evident to the beginner why a separate section of this book should be given to explaining the size of types, but when he is shown, for example, a line of 12 pt. Plantin 110 beside a line of 12 pt. Centaur he is likely to think that the 12 pt. Plantin is at least a 'size' larger than the Centaur. Beginners are confounded by the lack of logical relationship between the apparent size of a type and its description in terms of points.

When a type is described as being 12 pt. or 24 pt. it is not the size of letter (face) which is being described but a dimension of the body. Reference to the diagram on page 10 will make this clear. Thus 12 pt. type means that the body from front (where the nick is) to the back (the opposite side of the prismatic body) is 12 pts. Thinking of the body as a platform from which rises the face supported by a bevel (neck or beard), any convenient-sized letter may be cast on that body. It is now quite common for a letter which would normally be called 10 pt. to be cast on a 12 pt. body, hence the expression 'This book is printed in Baskerville 10 on 12,' meaning a normal 10 pt. is cast on a 12 pt. body. Casting a letter on a larger body has the same effect as leading.

From the above it follows that when a size of type is mentioned without the name or series number, no clear or definite idea of the size of the letter is given. The difference in appearance between types of the same body dimension is clearly demonstrated by the lines, all in 12 pt., on opposite page.

The length of line taken up by each alphabet also draws attention to the 'set' of the type which is the dimension at right angles to the point-wise dimension. It will be seen how great is the variation in set, so that a long-alphabet type like Scotch or Plantin or Baskerville is the publisher's friend when he has a manuscript which is short and he wishes to make it appear good value for money. (It is a pity the public are still inclined to judge the value of a book by its bulk.) On the other hand, if the manuscript is long and the paper short, the publisher would be wise to use Bembo or Fournier which is particularly economical of space.

Another warning to the beginner is not to expect the same amount of increase between one size and another when one type family is compared with another type family. For example, there appears to be a great increase in weight between 24 pt. and 30 pt. Perpetua which is not noticeable in Bembo.

This is largely due to the varying X-height which is the distance between the mean-line and the base-line. 'It is easily seen that even though the base-line may remain constant in relation to the body, the mean-line can be placed any distance above, according to the designer's wish. For technical convenience many types are cast with a uniform beard for certain groups or sizes, but it results in the descenders of some sizes being uncomfortably abbreviated. The three positions of the base line most generally adopted are known as 'common line', 'titling line', 'script line'.

Titling means that the letters, always capitals, are cast 'full face' on the body; there are therefore no related lower-case letters. Strictly speaking, the letter is not quite full face on the body. That is, a 72 pt. titling type does not have a face which is exactly 72 pt. but about 0.014 in. less, owing to the impossibility of casting a letter satisfactorily without a bevel.

Beginners often assume that because a type is obtainable in one size, it should be available in all other sizes. This is not so. An unusual, fancy or decorative letter might only be manufactured in one or two sizes. If it proved popular, other sizes might be added later, but for a time and maybe for ever only one or two sizes would be at the service of the typographer. Nearly all popular designs are made in the following sizes, and the student can expect these sizes to be manufactured even though one printer may not possess all of them. Starting from the smallest sizes they are 6, 8, 10, 12, 14, 18, 24, 30, 36, 42, 48, 60, 72 pt. It will be noticed that the intervals are of 2 points in the smaller sizes, 6 points in the medium sizes, and 12 points in the larger sizes. Above 30 pt. it is rare to find any intermediate sizes other than those mentioned, but at the lower end of the scale it is becoming increasingly common to find printers with 7, 9 and 11 pt., while 13 and 16 pt. are rare.

Times Roman, which was originally designed for the use of the newspaper, *The Times*, has a range of sizes starting with 4¼ pt. and including 5½ and 6½ pt. as well as those already mentioned, but the student typographer should find out from a typefounder's specimen book whether a particular size is made before specifying it on a layout. Times Roman is almost alone in its wide range of small sizes which are adapted to the special circumstances of a newspaper, and it is unwise for the student to think he might be able to get such a range of sizes in another design.

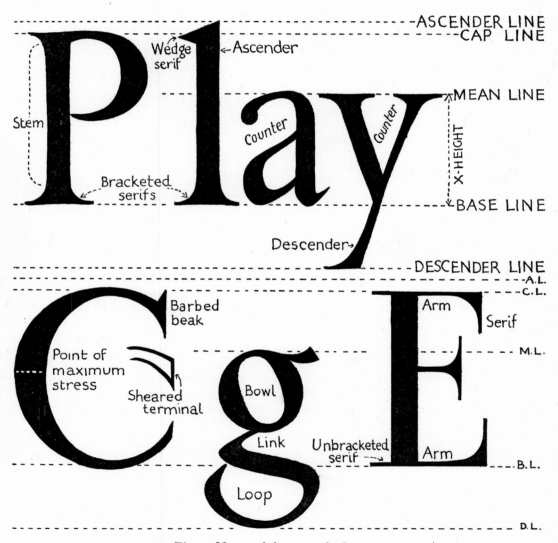

Fig. 4. Names of the parts of a letter.

It is far wiser to think of a normal range of sizes, as that given above, with the possibility of it being supplemented by 7, 9 and 11 pt.

Larger than 72 pt., one occasionally comes across 84 and 96 pt. type cast in metal. A wood letter is more usual; that is, the printing stamp is made of wood (usually boxwood) instead of metal. The sizes are generally in multiples of pica (12 pts.) which is referred to as a line, hence a size will be known as 6 line, meaning that the point dimension of the body is 6 lines of 12 pt. (72 pt.), and as most wood letter is titling it means that the letter will be almost 72 pt. from cap-line to base-line.

ABCDEFGHIJKLMNOPQRSTUVWXYZ SCOTCH 46
abcdefghijklmnopqrstuvwxyz
ABCDEFGHIJKLMNOPQRSTUVWXYZ
abcdefghijklmnopqrstuvwxyz

ABCDEFGHIJKLMNOPQRSTUVWXYZ TIMES 327
abcdefghijklmnopqrstuvwxyz
ABCDEFGHIJKLMNOPQRSTUVWXYZ
abcdefghijklmnopqrstuvwxyz

ABCDEFGHIJKLMNOPQRSTUVWXYZ PLANTIN 110
abcdefghijklmnopqrstuvwxyz
ABCDEFGHIJKLMNOPQRSTUVWXYZ
abcdefghijklmnopqrstuvwxyz

ABCDEFGHIJKLMNOPQRSTUVWXYZ BODONI 135
abcdefghijklmnopqrstuvwxyz
ABCDEFGHIJKLMNOPQRSTUVWXYZ
abcdefghijklmnopqrstuvwxyz

ABCDEFGHIJKLMNOPQRSTUVWXYZ GARAMOND 156
abcdefghijklmnopqrstuvwxyz
ABCD EFGHIJKLMNOP QRSTUVWXYZ
abcdefghijklmnopqrstuvwxyz

ABCDEFGHIJKLMNOPQRSTUVWXYZ BASKERVILLE 169
abcdefghijklmnopqrstuvwxyz
ABCDEFGHIJKLMNOPQRSTUVWXYZ
abcdefghijklmnopqrstuvwxyz

ABCDEFGHIJKLMNOPQRSTUVWXYZ BEMBO 270
abcdefghijklmnopqrstuvwxyz
ABCDEFGHIJKLMNOPQRSTUVWXYZ
abcdefghijklmnopqrstuvwxyz

ABCDEFGHIJKLMNOPQRSTUVWXYZ PERPETUA 239
abcdefghijklmnopqrstuvwxyz
ABCDEFGHIJKLMNOPQRSTUVWXYZ
abcdefghijklmnopqrstuvwxyz

Fig. 5. A comparison of 12pt. Types demonstrating that the size of type when given in points may mean a different APPEARING size in different type designs.

Legibility and Readability

A QUESTION students frequently ask of an instructor, or of themselves, is 'How may I know a good type when I see one?' Once you are agreed as to what a thing is for, the goodness or success of the thing will depend on whether or not it fulfils the purpose for which it is intended.

What is type for? Obviously to read, and to read with as little discomfort on the part of the reader as possible. But reading at different times is carried on under different circumstances, and the qualities desired on one occasion might be irrelevant on another. For example, in an advertisement, one or two words might reasonably and appropriately be in a bold or decorative or flourished letter in order to attract attention. But the very qualities which are successful on such an occasion would be quite out of place in a book where continuous reading is the intention. So there are different criteria for judging book faces from the remainder which may be called 'jobbing', 'display' or 'advertising' faces. In their nature most advertising types are ephemeral and are quickly changed. Lasting beauty is rarely sought and still more rarely attained, and as this book is intended for beginners who need to have a high standard put before them by which to judge letters, only those which have the authority of a good tradition are recommended as a first study.

Letters of an alphabet are arbitrary symbols representing the sounds of speech and their efficiency as such depends on everybody, after having learned them, being able to recognise them instantly. And as we recognise most quickly those things with which we are most familiar, it follows that letters with which we are familiar are, to that extent, more legible than unfamiliar forms. There is much more to legibility than familiarity, but familiarity, which might be called normality, is certainly one of the most important factors in legibility. In order that a type may be legible, in the sense that it may be easily read with the least fatigue on the part of the reader, it must be familiar in general shape and proportion. Scientists have devised many tests of legibility, one of which is the 'blink test'. It has been found that as the eyes become tired or strained the rate of involuntary blinking increases so that, other things being equal, the frequency of blinking will give a numerical comparison of the fatigue incurred. Thus, under fixed conditions of light, distance, etc., types may be compared; and a type producing a high blink rate is assumed to be less legible than one which can be read without much blinking.

It has also been found that the eyes, in reading, move along the line in a series of leaps, with moments of rest, or 'fixation' as the scientists call it, in between. This requires continual adjustment of the muscles of the eyes which in reading are generally only a foot or eighteen inches from the book. Fourteen inches is about ideal for people with normal eyesight. The eyes are more naturally adjusted to focus on objects five feet or more distant, and anything nearer requires fatiguing adjustment. Blinking has been found to act as a rest for the muscles of the eyes and reduces fatigue. Also as the mechanisms of the eyes are at rest when viewing distant objects, an occasional glance out of the window will relieve the strain of reading just as changing one's grip in carrying a heavy travelling bag brings relief. As it is the moments of fixation, when the eyes are compelled to perform the tiresome task of near vision, that are fatiguing, it follows that any unusual or distracting features which tend to increase the periods of fixation and interrupt the rhythmic movement of the eyes are likely to induce fatigue.

In general, the investigations of scientists and occulists have only endorsed by experiment the principles evolved intuitively by type designers and typographers throughout the centuries. But before we go any further, let us be a little clearer as to what is meant by legibility, readability and visibility. Letterers, typographers and writers on these matters use these terms in slightly different senses. One reason for the different shades of meaning is the almost inseparable fusion of utilitarian and aesthetic elements in letter forms and their arrangement. This leads some writers to distinguish between legibility, as meaning that the forms can be seen and comprehended, and readability, as meaning that an inviting, pleasant or aesthetic quality is added to the mere recognisability. In this sense it would be possible to describe a type as being legible but not readable.

A comparison might be made with a drinking vessel. From a purely utilitarian point of view anything which will hold the liquid and convey it to our lips fulfils its purpose. Yet who but a starving man could enjoy his tea or beer from a rough tin can, and it is a dull clod who does not enjoy it more when taken from a cup or tankard of elegant shape, inviting colour and smooth texture? Here again, scientific experiment has proved that pleasure in food and drink is more than an epicure's fad, but a positive aid to digestion by stimulating the production of digestive juices. Thus it is fair to say that a drink from a well-designed mug is likely to be more readily digested than one taken from an ugly container.

Some writers contend that beauty and legibility are so inextricably intermingled that without beauty a letter cannot be legible. In order to avoid the controversies which arise with the use of the word beauty and the jargon of aesthetics, the word visibility has been employed to describe what in typography might be compared with a drinking vessel's bare ability to convey a liquid to the mouth; readability in type being parallel to the quality in a mug from which one drinks with pleasure or even enthusiasm.

From now on we shall consider the factors which contribute to readability, and only letters that are reasonably visible will be considered. Again science underlines traditional practice. In order to be visible only, apart from being readable, every letter in an alphabet must be sufficiently different to avoid the possibility of one letter being mistaken for another. There should be some contrast between thick and thin strokes (fats and leans, as Moxon calls them) but not too much contrast. There should be a just and true proportion between the width and height of the stem. Too great a thickness of stem makes the general effect too dark, as the clarity of the letters individually, as well as in the mass, depends on an adequate amount of background showing. If the stem thickness is too light, the effect is too grey and the eye is strained by the need to distinguish the shapes of words from the general grey blur. At this juncture it must be pointed out that experiments have proved that we read, not so much by apprehending every letter separately,

but in words or even groups of words, recognising them by their general shape. Hence a letter must be judged not by itself alone, but by how it combines with other letters in the mass.

Because of the fact that we read by the general shapes of words, lower-case is more readable in the mass than capitals owing to the variety of word silhouettes made by ascenders and descenders. A novel set throughout in capitals would present a visual task few people would care to undertake. For the same reason variety in the width of letters is as vital to visibility as it is indispensable to readability. The tendency towards uniformity in width of letters which is exhibited in some of the so-called Gothic types, not only results in a loss of aesthetic appeal, but in visibility. In these types certain words have to be deciphered by reference to context, the shapes themselves being unreadable. It is also demonstrable that the upper half of letters is more readable than the lower half. The student can prove this for himself by covering up with a piece of plain paper the lower half of a line of letters, and the words will be reasonably legible, but if the upper half is covered, the lower half is usually unintelligible.

Readability depends on many more factors than the shapes and proportions of the letters, fundamental as they are. Size is obviously important and there is no doubt that any size less than 12 pt. produces strain of some degree, though practical conditions so often make the larger, more readable, size impossible.

Next there must be sufficient brightness of reading material—that is, the inked portions must be in marked contrast to the paper. Neither the ink nor the paper should be glossy. The black should be of the blackest and the paper white. Tinted, creamy or off-white paper may have aesthetic appeal but it does not increase visibility. On the other hand, there is no evidence that slight tinting decreases visibility, and therefore, off-white papers may be used without fear of reducing readability. The type itself should be clearly and crisply printed so that the shapes are not blurred by faulty inking and impression. The brightness of the area surrounding the reading material affects the readability and should not be very different in intensity. Shiny glass-topped desks are undesirable, while on the other hand, too dark surroundings are harmful.

The space between the lines, known as leading, has a considerable influence on the ease with which a type is read. Most types are made more readable by judicious leading. A closely related factor is the length of line in any given size. The length of line will depend on the size of type but the principle can be expressed in this way, that, other things being equal, a line should not contain more than about ten to twelve average-length words.

Finally, for comfortable reading, there should be adequate margins and reasonable rest periods.

All the foregoing factors are always present in some degree so that it is by no means easy to decide what precisely makes a type legible, as so many factors are involved *simultaneously*. On this subject, Frederick W. Goudy, perhaps the most prolific type designer the world has known, with over a hundred types to his credit, has said: 'As to legibility, I shall not here comment. Everyone knows (or thinks he knows) just what constitutes it; I fear I do not, or I would never permit myself consciously to make a type that was not a quintessence of legibility.'

It has now been shown that legibility depends on many simultaneous conditions, but there are a few well established devices in designing letters to overcome certain optical illusions. If all letters were made exactly equal in height they would not appear even, but round or pointed letters would appear shorter. The diagram will show more clearly than words can describe how the lower-case t must be thicker towards the base of the stem in order to avoid the appearance of falling backwards. Round letters need to 'go over the line' more at the bottom than the top; the dot of the i must not be exactly over the centre of the stem to appear so. The strokes of the W must be slightly curved at the lower extremities in order that they may seem to be straight. The point of maximum stress in round letters needs to be slightly greater than the thickness of the stems of straight letters in order to appear the same thickness. Most letters need some modification of

this kind in order to give a regular appearance.

Modifications of proportion are necessary when a letter design is made in different sizes not merely for aesthetic reasons but for legibility's sake. An obvious and easily understood example is that of lower-case e. In a size 24 pt. or over it would be quite legible for the cross-bar of the lower-case e to be at one-third or less of its height and still have an appreciable and printable counter. But imagine the same letter in 6 pt. type. The total height of the lower-case e cannot be more than about 4 points and may be less. One-third of this will be only just over a point (1/72 in.) which means the counter will almost disappear or be so small that it will easily fill with ink and be mistaken for a c. To overcome this, the height of the cross-bar is lowered in the smaller sizes to give the maximum counter and therefore the maximum differentiation from c and o, with which an e might occasionally be confused. The same applies to the bowl of lower-case a.

We have said elsewhere that the distance from base-line to mean-line is known to founders as the X-height. The X-height in the smaller sizes is increased to maintain legibility, which is of supreme importance in sizes below 10 point. Beauty of drawing of individual characters can scarcely be thought of in these sizes, but legibility is paramount. Not only is the X-height generally increased as the sizes get smaller, but the difference between thick and thin stroke may be less pronounced. Thus a hairline one-tenth the thickness of the stem, which would be ample in a large size, would almost disappear when reduced to 6 point. The hairline is therefore thickened somewhat and may be a quarter or even a third of the thickness of the stem. Serifs, also, are best thickened slightly in the smaller sizes. These general principles are borne out by the fact that the most demonstrably legible of small types are those which have little contrast between thick and thin strokes, strong serifs and clear distinguishing features in letters like a, c, e.

At the other end of the scale, in sizes from 18 pt. up, legibility is not such a dominating factor. It would be an ill-designed letter indeed, of 18 pt. or larger, that could not be read at normal distances. Beauty of shape can be thought of without fear of the letter becoming illegible, and one of the most obvious ways of improving the shape (as compared with the smaller sizes) is to decrease the X-height. Both thick and thin strokes can be more slender, and curves can be drawn with all the subtle artistry of which the designer is capable.

In a way, sizes from 16 pt. up are judged by different criteria from those applied to type from 14 pt. down. Broadly, one might say that technical considerations hold the field in the smaller sizes but give way to artistic considerations when dealing with large letters. A small type must be judged on its appearance in the mass, while larger sizes must be considered in lines and words and even as individual letters having an abstract beauty of their own.

With such different standards of judgment it is small wonder that many typefounders in the past issued certain designs of letter in small sizes only and other designs in large sizes only. Today type users expect to have a letter in sizes from 6 pt. to 72 pt., every size being an obvious member of one family and of the same parentage. In the past, when punches were cut by hand, the punch-cutter modified the letter to suit the size he was cutting to such an extent that today we would hardly regard some sizes as belonging to the same family.

Uniformity of character, or rather family likeness, through a range of sizes is now aimed at, but this means a different master design for at least three groups of sizes, small, medium and large. More groups, each with a modified design, is better, and one authority says that each size should have its own special design.

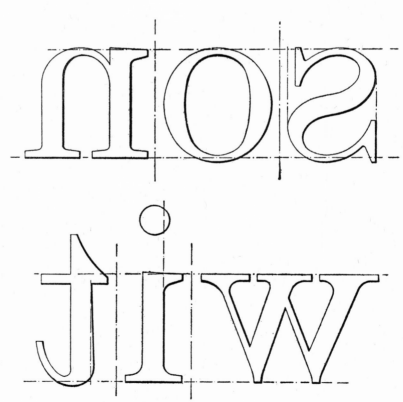

Fig. 6. How geometric accuracy in letters is modified to give an appearance of evenness.

The Classification of Type Faces

THERE is as yet no universally agreed classification of type faces. Those that have appeared are mainly historical in grouping, or are genealogical showing the growth of one out of another. The classification here presented is made from the point of view of the beginner who is faced with a large number of varying forms of the roman alphabet cast as type, and who needs to arrange them in an intelligible and significant order as an aid to study.

The method of science is to divide things into a few immense groups that are then broken up into smaller groups. In the larger groups, many things which seem on the surface to be very different from one another will be found under one heading. Thus a whale, which lives in the sea is not a fish but a mammal, and forms of life as dissimilar as an elephant, an eagle and an eel come under the one heading of vertebrates, the animal kingdom being divided into vertebrates and invertebrates.

It seems reasonable to divide our normal roman letters into the two main groups of serifed letters and unserifed letters. The serifed letters might then be broken up into sections for which there are a sufficient number of letter designs having sufficiently distinguishable characteristics. The best way of doing this seems to be according to the nature of the serifs, though there may be other features which need to be taken into account when placing a given letter design into one of the three groups here decided upon. The old-face and modern groups present no difficulty and these are clearly defined both by word and diagram on pages 18-19. The slab-serif group presents a problem because it brings together the Venetian group of types which are traditional book types, and advertising types like Playbill which could never be satisfactorily used in quantities greater than a few words. Nevertheless, our classification is according to the nature of the serif, not according to the purpose for which the letter is employed. The Venetian group certainly has slab serifs, though added to a letter formation with curves stressed as in old face, so that the beginner might think of a Venetian as a slab-serifed old face.

Some of the slab-serifed letters look more like block letters (monotone) to which slab serifs have

SANSERIF (Block, Gothic, Grotesque)

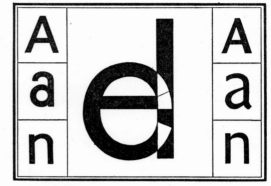

1. As the name implies—absence of serifs.
2. Usually no difference, or little difference, in thickness between the strokes which are normally thick and those normally thin.

Good Sans types are Gill Sans, Cable, Erbar, Johnston's Underground Sans, Grotesque No. 9.

Fig. 7.

been added, in contrast to the Venetian, looking like slab serifs added to an old face, although Venetian style came before old face.

The French Antique group comprises those types in which the slab serif is deeper than the

SLAB SERIF (Egyptian)

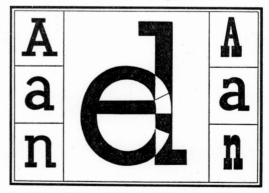

1. The serifs about the same thickness as the stems.
2. Usually the serifs are unbracketed.
3. Sometimes, as in Playbill, the serifs are thicker than the stems.
4. Generally a 'monotone', that is, having all the strokes the same thickness.

Some Slab-Serif types are Beton, Rockwell, Scarab.

Fig. 8.

thickness of the stem, and is a letter form that has been very popular in advertising for the last 20 years or more. The use of these types is limited. For display lines in advertisements and on book jackets the strong tone and rich texture is admirable. Playbill is a member of this family.

Sanserif is a good descriptive term easily understood by the merest tyro, but the beginner has reason to be a little bewildered to find some sans types labelled Grotesque or Gothic. There seems nothing Gothic about these letters in the sense which is usually associated with that word— appertaining to the period and the culture between

name) may be ungainly, it seems a strain on the meaning of the word grotesque to apply it to a straightforward sanserif letter. Nevertheless, the words Gothic and Grotesque are still in general use in the printing trade and the apprentice typographer is warned that when he vaguely asks for a gothic letter (intending black-letter or what the average layman calls Old English) he may be given a sanserif.

Latin is another minor group of types, in which the serifs are triangular.

Apart from the normal roman there are such letters as Gothic (black-letter) and Script which

OLD FACE (Diagonal Stress)

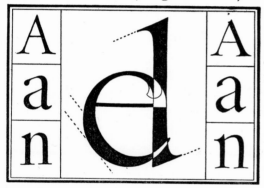

1. Point of maximum stress at an angle.
2. Gradual transition from thick to thin strokes.
3. Little contrast between thick and thin strokes (there are exceptions).
4. Serifs bracketed.
5. Serifs of lower-case letters like d, b, n, m, etc., at an angle (see diagram).

Good Old Face types are Bembo, Caslon Old Face, Garamond, Plantin.

Fig. 9.

MODERN FACE (Vertical Stress)

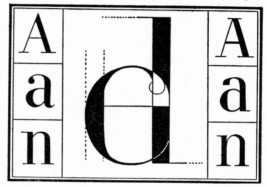

1. Point of maximum stress vertical.
2. Abrupt transition from thick to thin strokes.
3. Strong contrast between thick and thin strokes (hairlines).
4. Serifs usually (but not always) unbracketed.
5. Serifs of lower-case letters like d, b, l, etc., horizontal.

Good Modern Face types are Bodoni, Walbaum, Bell, Scotch Roman.

Fig. 10.

about 1200 and 1500. The beginner is justified in feeling that there is nothing in common between a Gothic church like Salisbury Cathedral and a Gothic sanserif type. There is indeed no way in which the beauty of the one can be compared with the plainness of the other, and one can only hope that some day this inept application of the word will be abandoned.

Grotesque is a scarcely more apt term, because though many 'Grots' (they deserve such a nick-

require a group to themselves, and then there are the freaks and fancies that have been by some critics grouped under the word 'exotics' which at least describes their abnormal nature. But the word exotic has also been used to describe foreign types such as Greek, Russian, Arabic, etc.

In conclusion, though it is wise to be systematic in study, the student is advised not to worry unduly whether such-and-such a type belongs to this or that group. Classification is largely the librarian's job, and designers rarely think in terms of classification when creating a new design. The designer, working within the inevitable tradition of the forms of letters, is guided by the use to which his work is to be put and his own aesthetic intuitions. Only afterwards will the question of classification arise. The value of the study of classification to the beginner is largely the training in analysis, that is, in distinguishing how one type differs from another.

A CLASSIFICATION
OF ROMAN TYPE FACES

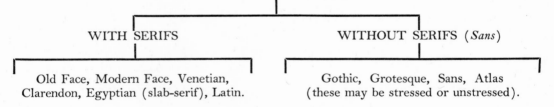

ROMAN LETTERS

All the letters we generally use are Roman or its derivatives. The word "Roman" is also used to distinguish upright letters from sloping. Sloping letters are usually called italic or cursive. This classification applies to Roman letters in both senses of the word.

WITH SERIFS	WITHOUT SERIFS (*Sans*)
Old Face, Modern Face, Venetian, Clarendon, Egyptian (slab-serif), Latin.	Gothic, Grotesque, Sans, Atlas (these may be stressed or unstressed).

This is OLD FACE

This is MODERN FACE

This is VENETIAN

This is CLARENDON

This is EGYPTIAN (slab-serif)

This is LATIN

This is GOTHIC

This is GROTESQUE

This is SANS

This is ATLAS

As letters with serifs comprise the far larger and most important group it will be helpful to the student to sub-divide the serifed letters into three main groups of 'Old Face,' 'Modern,' and 'Slab Serif' according to the nature of the serifs, even though it will mean letters being put under one heading that are used for very different purposes and which have a different history.

Fig. 11.

IT is important for the student typographer to differentiate between 'founders'' type; 'MONO-TYPE', which is produced on an apparatus which casts and sets individual types; and 'slug-set' type where each line of type is cast in one solid piece or 'slug'.

Founders' type is made of the hardest of printing-type metals. All type metals contain lead, tin, antimony, and often a little copper. Lead comprises the bulk of the alloy which on its own would be much too soft. The addition of tin, antimony and copper increases the hardness and sharpness of the shape when cast, but this harder metal needs to be cast much slower than softer metals. Founders' type, then, is made of the finest metal with less lead and more tin and antimony. It is very accurately made and to a good craftsman is certainly the best type to handle. But it must be set by hand, which rules out the use of founders' type for the text of a long book unless it is for a *de luxe* edition where cost is comparatively important.

Firms of typefounders cast the type and supply printers with a fount or font (originally fund) of type. A fount is a complete set of letters and characters which are necessary to set continuous reading matter, which includes not only the letters of the alphabet in CAPITALS, lower-case, SMALL CAPS, *ITALIC CAPS* and *italic lower-case*, but such signs as commas, question marks, apostrophes, hyphens, and logotypes such as ffi, fl. Printers are naturally reluctant to buy a fount of type unless there is a good chance of it being adequately employed. Many type designs are obtainable from founders only and are there-fore only available for hand-setting, which limits the occasions and extent of their use.

'MONOTYPE' needs more explaining because the term is used loosely in the trade though the meaning will always be clear to the initiated from the context.

'MONOTYPE' is a registered trade name for a machine which casts single letters at a remarkably high speed, in the correct order and arrangement for printing. The majority of books today are set on these marvellous machines which noisily deliver in a column of the correct width, the type from which to print. The process of pro-ducing type on the 'MONOTYPE' is divided into two stages. First the keyboard which resembles an ordinary office typewriter with a greater abundance of keys. As these keys are operated, very much as a typewriter is operated with the fingers, holes are punched in a roll of paper about 5 in. wide. A different arrangement of holes corresponds to each letter of the alphabet and the rest of the miscellaneous sorts. When the operator has finished 'typing' the copy, the roll will be seen punched with a series of holes in different positions and in general, will look like a small pianola roll.

Fig. 12. *Monotype Keyboard.*

This roll is placed in another machine called the caster, which, as the name implies, actually casts the type. As the roll passes over a perfor-ated cylinder, compressed air passes through the holes in the paper and sets in motion a mechanism that casts the letter corresponding to the holes in the paper. As these holes correspond with the letters of the copy, it follows that the letters cast will be identical with the copy. Thus every letter of the author's manuscript is cast successively in metal. The operator judges when it is necessary to break words at the end of lines, and a mechanical device puts the same amount of space between every word in each line.

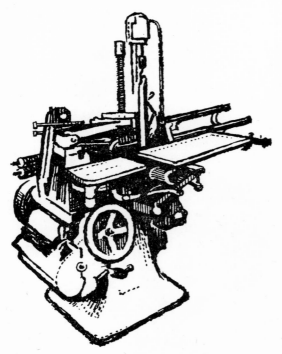

Fig. 13. *Monotype Caster.*

Strictly, then, 'MONOTYPE' is the name of a machine, but people speak of the type designs available for use on this machine as 'MONOTYPES'. Hence a man may be heard to say 'Bembo is a 'MONOTYPE' but the original Caslon Old Face is a founders' type'. He might also be heard to put it this way, 'Bembo is a face that is only available on the Mono (short for 'MONOTYPE') and cannot be obtained in founders' type'.

Most medium sized printing firms possess a 'MONOTYPE' machine. In order to produce type with such a machine, a complete set of matrices of every letter and sort will be required. The printer will own sets of matrices of the types he likes or believes his clients will like, and in the sizes he knows are most generally useful. But other type designs or other sizes he may acquire in two ways. Either by hiring the matrices and casting the type on his own machines or by purchasing the type from a 'trade typesetter' who casts a variety of types to serve many printers.

The metal used for casting the type for continuous composition of a manuscript is considerably softer than founders' type metal. There is more lead and less tin, and owing to the speed at which it is cast, a greater likelihood of air bubbles weakening the structure. Nevertheless, it is generally very satisfactory and very long runs can be obtained from monotype, though not so long as those from founders' type.

When it is not required to set a continuous manuscript, the 'MONOTYPE' machine can be used to produce founts of type for hand-setting. For this purpose rather more tin is used to produce a somewhat harder metal, but again it is not so hard-wearing as founders' metal.

There are a number of trade typesetters who own a large number of matrices and machines for casting founts of type, as just described, that a printer can buy at a reasonable price. Single words or small groups of words can be bought in this way so that a printer, who does not himself possess a wide range of types, can economically extend his range of display types by purchases for special occasions from the trade typesetter.

Most of the best type designs readily available for setting books are produced on the 'MONOTYPE'; and through trade setters, anybody can expect to have his work set in a well-designed type face. Moreover, when for economic reasons the text of a job may have to be set in a type the printer has in stock, it is not unreasonable to ask for display lines to be bought specially.

To sum up, the word 'MONOTYPE' may have three different senses: (1) 'MONOTYPE', the machine itself; (2) 'MONOTYPE', the metal types; (3) the type-face designs. In this latter sense the Monotype Corporation who manufacture the machine entitle a very useful publication of theirs 'A Desk Book of 'MONOTYPE' Faces'.

'Linotype' is also a trade name for a type-casting machine which, as the name suggests, casts 'a line o' type' in one piece instead of letter-for-letter. The Intertype and the Ludlow are two other machines which in their different ways cast a line of type. For the layman, the Linotype and the Intertype machines may be regarded as identical, but the Ludlow is different mechanically and in the method of its operation.

Fig. 14. *Linotype machine.*

The Linotype, like the 'MONOTYPE' machine, has a keyboard resembling a many-keyed type-writer but it is attached to the casting mechanism instead of being separated as a distinct machine. As the operator presses the keys the matrices of the characters are released in turn and fall into line until the required length is reached. The whole line of matrices is then swung into position over a nozzle through which molten type metal is pumped making a cast in one piece or 'slug' of

the complete line of type. This is then cooled with water and delivered into a tray for later removal. Only a matter of seconds elapses between the time when the operator finishes 'tapping-out' the letters on the keyboard and the delivery of a slug ready for printing. The text of nearly all newspapers is set on the Lino-type or Intertype.

In order to cast letters, or rather lines of letters, at such a speed, the metal must contain an even higher proportion of lead, which means a softer, quicker-wearing type. There is a danger of air bubbles in the metal and an uneven height to the letters, but under the best conditions the results are astonishingly good.

As far as the design of the faces are concerned some designs are only available on the Linotype —Granjon, for example. There are a few designs which are available on both Mono and Lino (to use the day-to-day jargon of printers), e.g., Times Roman. On the other hand, the student will find that the typefounders, 'MONOTYPE' and Linotype all have a type named Bodoni, but he will find that each company's version of Bodoni is slightly different.

The names given to types are sometimes mis-leading to beginners who might think that 'MONOTYPE' Caslon is the same as founders' Caslon Old Face; there is a Linotype version, and one produced by the American typefounders. It is true that all these types are very similar and have a common origin, but a trained eye will not hesitate to pronounce the original founders' Caslon as being the best of the bunch.

The student is also warned that besides the beautiful and useful Baskerville ('MONOTYPE' Series 169) which is one of the best book types in general use today, there is an admirable Linotype version but an execrable one produced by the founders which does not deserve the honoured name of Baskerville. On the other hand, Messrs. Stephenson Blake produce Fry's Baskerville which is a beauty.

This is Plantin 110 which looks its best on art paper or any smooth-surfaced paper. Compare it with Caslon which looks spidery on art paper but gains in character on antique or rough surfaced paper. *Here is a line of italic for comparison.*

This is Caslon Old Face which was designed at a time when printing was done on a hand-press on damp hand-made paper. Caslon looks its best when conditions are near those for which it was designed. *Here is a line of italic for comparison.*

Here you see Gill Sans the aristocrat of the Sans group of types—if one can think of anything being aristocratic among such a work-a-day lot of type faces. Note its behaviour on the different papers. *Here is a line of italic for comparison.*

Here is Bodoni a typical ' Modern ' face though it was designed before 1800. Bodoni is somewhat mechanical looking as though drawn with ruler and compass, all trace of calligraphy having disappeared. But it is appropriate on some occasions. *Here is a line of italic for comparison.*

You are now reading Rockwell type which can be very useful in advertising. The range of weights and together with the ' Shadow ' version seen on page 116 are an advantage in some kinds of commercial work.

This is Baskerville type, Monotype series No 169. It is a modern re-cutting of an 18th century letter. Its unaffected simplicity make it useful for a wide variety of purposes. Because it has both Old Face and Modern characteristics it is described as a 'transitional' design.

This is Bembo, a beautiful ' old face ' type which, though intended for use on antique papers, retains a surprising amount of 'colour' and character on art paper. Bembo is almost the ideal ' book ' face.

Cloister, which you are now reading, being fairly strong in 'colour,' does not look so anaemic as many 15th century revivals are apt to look on art paper. Of course, it at its best on hand made paper.

This is Plantin 110 which looks its best on art paper or any smooth-surfaced paper. Compare it with Caslon which looks spidery on art paper but gains in character on antique or rough surfaced paper. *Here is a line of italic for comparison.*

This is Caslon Old Face which was designed at a time when printing was done on a hand-press on damp hand-made paper. Caslon looks its best when conditions are near those for which it was designed. *Here is a line of italic for comparison.*

Here you see Gill Sans the aristocrat of the Sans group of types—if one can think of anything being aristocratic among such a work-a-day lot of type faces. Note its behaviour on the different papers. *Here is a line of italic for comparison.*

Here is Bodoni a typical 'Modern' face though it was designed before 1800. Bodoni is somewhat mechanical looking as though drawn with ruler and compass, all trace of calligraphy having disappeared. But it is appropriate on some occasions. *Here is a line of italic for comparison.*

You are now reading Rockwell type which can be very useful in advertising. The range of weights and together with the ' Shadow ' version seen on page 116 are an advantage in some kinds of commercial work.

This is Baskerville type, Monotype series No 169. It is a modern re-cutting of an 18th century letter. Its unaffected simplicity make it useful for a wide variety of purposes. Because it has both Old Face and Modern characteristics it is described as a 'transitional' design.

This is Bembo, a beautiful 'old face' type which, though intended for use on antique papers, retains a surprising amount of 'colour' and character on art paper. Bembo is almost the ideal 'book' face.

Cloister, which you are now reading, being fairly strong in 'colour,' does not look so anaemic as many 15th century revivals are apt to look on art paper. Of course, it at its best on hand made paper.

Fig. 15. *Fascia board by Eric Gill for Douglas Cleverdon's shop in Bristol. Gill Sans type is derived from this letter.*

Matrix   Punch

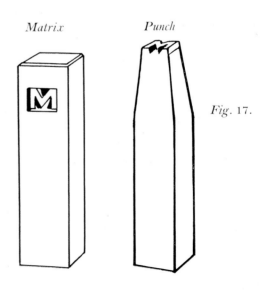

Fig. 17.

Fig. 16. *A punch cutter at work.*

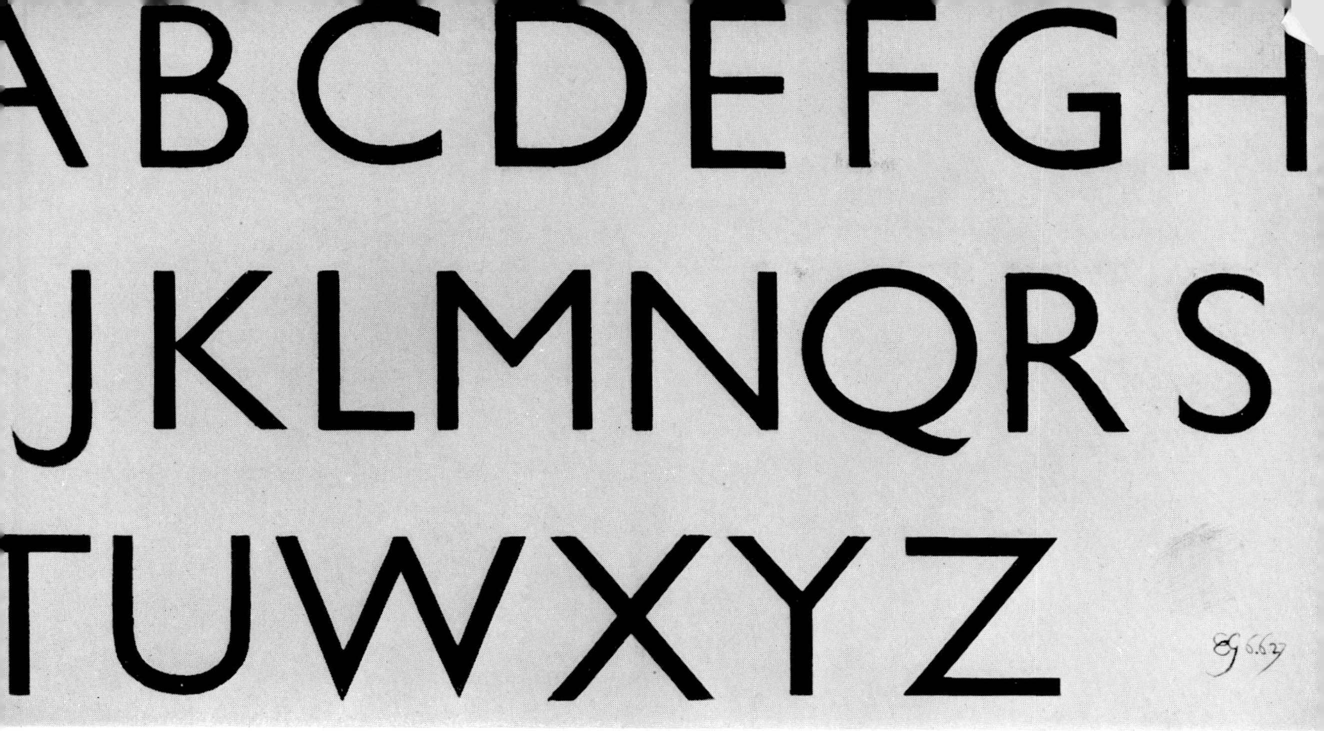
ABCDEFGH
JKLMNQRS
TUWXYZ

Figs. 18 and 19. Eric Gill's original designs for Gill Sans.

by Courtesy of the Monotype Corporation

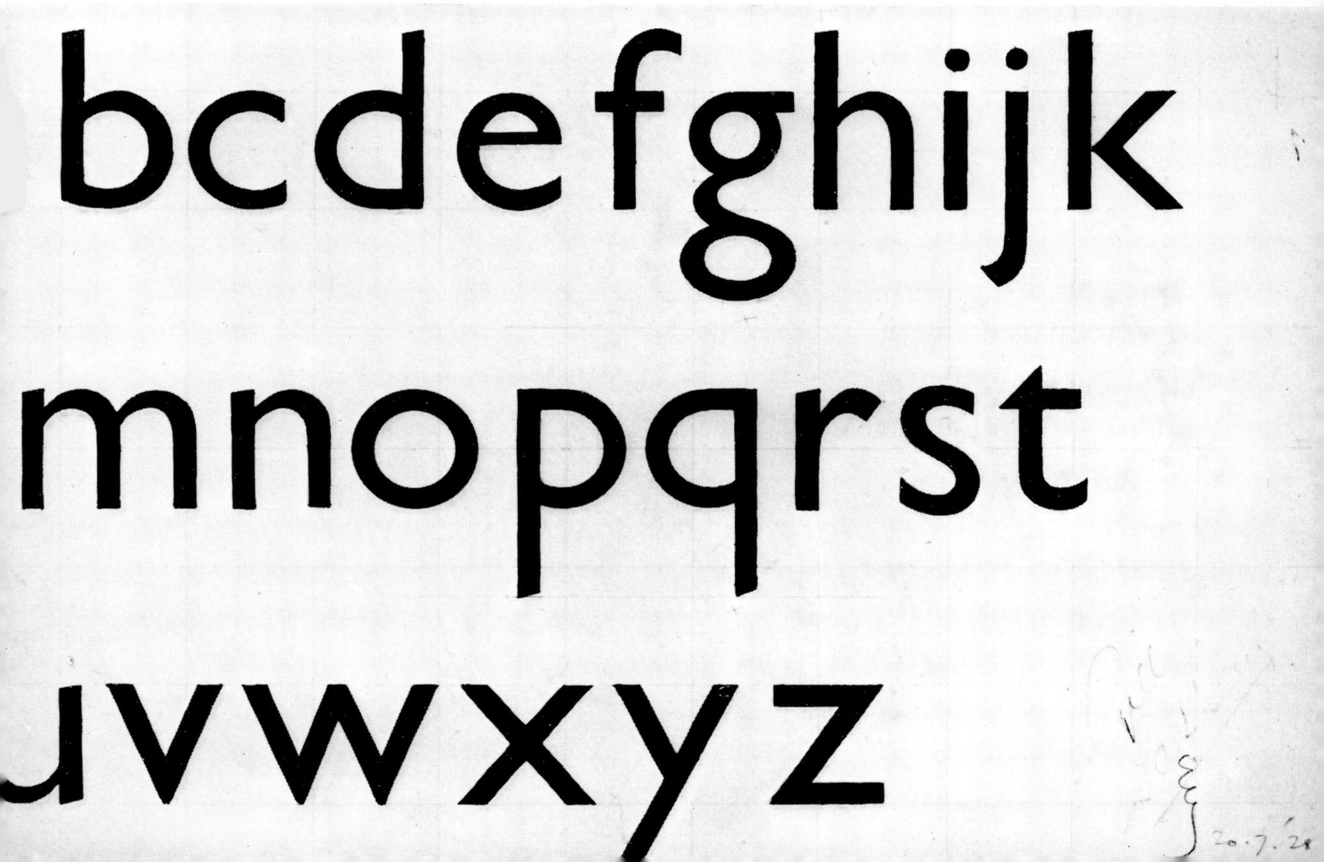
bcdefghijk
mnopqrst
vwxyz

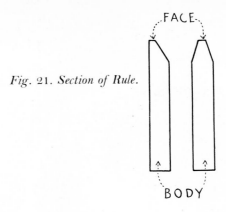

Fig. 21. Section of Rule.

Fig. 20. Pencil drawings of letters by Eric Gill.

THE word 'rules' in this sense does not mean a code of regulations by which printers conduct their business, but is the name applied to strips of brass or typemetal, the same height as type, and which print as straight lines. These vary in width from a very fine line, appropriately known as hairline rule, to broad bands 18 points or more in width.

As the very finest rules are too thin for the body to be the same thickness as the face, they are manufactured on thicker bodies. Some rules are made with the printing surface or face rising centrally over the body, but some rise vertically from one side of the body with the bevel on the other side. The diagram (*opposite*) will make this quite clear. They are known respectively as centre-face and side-face. Body sizes are generally 1, 1½, 2, 3, 4, 6, 8, 10, 12 and 18 pt., but face sizes vary considerably.

Rules made of brass are often manufactured so that the foot can be used to print from, that is, the rule can be used either way up. Thus, if you have a rule with a 1 pt. face on a 3 pt. body standing on one edge, it will print a line 1 pt. thick; upside down it will print a line 3 pts. thick. The examples above make this quite clear. Multiple rules are also obtainable where two or more thicknesses of rule are cast on one body.

Decorative rules are also in use, of which a few examples are given.

THESE little ornaments have been used by printers for centuries and some of the most delightful in use today are revivals of sixteenth-century designs. They are manufactured in exactly the same way as type, and are cast on similar bodies, with a nick on the front. They may be made in any of the normal type sizes, but the most usual ones are 6, 8, 10, 12, 18 and 24 pt. The larger sizes begin to lose the filigree charm of the sizes 12 pt. or less.

There is room for originality and taste in the selection and arrangement of fleurons which result in borders having a decorative quality which could scarcely be achieved in any other way. A few specimens are given in various sizes.

8 point borders

10 point borders

12 point borders

24 point borders

Fig. 22. ABOVE, *Flowers or Fleurons*
LEFT, *Printers' Rules*

Something About Paper

Why should an approach to type have a section devoted to paper? The experienced typographer knows only too well the importance of paper. 'The paper is part of the picture' was a slogan once used by a paper merchant in his advertising, and though most advertising must be taken with a pinch of salt, more than a pinch of salt in some cases, nevertheless the copywriter hit on an apt way of drawing attention to the importance of paper in printing. The layman would scarcely believe the difference paper will make to the appearance of a type design. The same type printed on different papers (see page 24) might seem like two different type designs. Even experts can be deceived. Type, then, cannot be studied apart from the paper it is printed on, and though it is not appropriate to describe the manufacture of paper in this book, the student of type is advised to become also a student of paper.

For the purpose of this book, and to avoid too many technicalities, papers may be thought of in two main groups—coated papers, that is, those papers which have a shiny surface of china clay, and which are absurdly called 'art' papers; and uncoated papers, that is, those without the china clay surface. Uncoated papers may be divided into rough and smooth, which correspond approximately to the terms used in the paper trade: 'antique' (rough) and calendered (smooth). Uncoated papers might also be thought of as hard sized and soft sized. Hard sized means that there is a comparatively large quantity of glue-size in or on it, making the paper less porous, firmer to touch, and giving it a pronounced 'rattle' when shaken. Soft sized means there is little size present, rendering the paper more porous, limp, and without the 'tinny' rattle of a hard-sized paper. All these things influence the appearance of the type and need to be considered to get the best out of a type design.

Rough or antique paper has a surface which, when magnified, is like a series of hillocks with valleys in between. In order to obtain a clean, sharp print, the type must be driven into the paper far enough for the tops of the hillocks to be squashed and also for the valleys to be filled with ink. The inked surface of the type will make a shallow trench or indentation in the paper, and inevitably, like the cream in the cream bun which oozes over the edges when the teeth press the top and bottom parts of the bun together, the ink will flow over the edge of the type and stain the sides of the indentation as well as the bottom. This will have the effect of thickening all the lines, blurring any refinements of form, and making the very fine lines of modern-face almost impossible to reproduce. Antique papers therefore demand an old-face type. Caslon Old Face does not look well on any paper but an antique. This is only natural, because Caslon was designed for printing on damp, hand-made paper in a screw press, which unavoidably thickens the strokes.

Modern-face types require for their proper rendering a smooth, but not coated, paper. Smooth paper will not require so much 'bump' or pressure in order to make every part of the type print with equal clarity and blackness. What is known as a 'kiss impression' will remove all the ink from the face of the type to the surface of the paper. No noticeable indentation will be made and no thickening of the strokes. A type will appear thinner and lighter when printed on a smooth paper than when printed on rough. Smooth paper will allow considerable refinements and subtleties of form to be plainly seen, and generally speaking, it is easier for the machine-minder.*

If the printing is to be done on rough paper

---

* The nomenclature of the printing industry is not altogether satisfactory in the words applied to craftsmen, as it is inept in the names of many types. Machine-minder does not suggest the great skill required to 'make ready,' that is, the operations carried out to obtain a clear and even impression of all the letters. The word minder makes one think of somebody who merely looks after a machine as a nanny looks after a child, and fails to give any idea of the skill and craftsmanship involved.

These craftsmen are also called pressmen, but reporters for newspapers are called pressmen. Printer is a good strong, straightforward, accurate word, but the proprietor or manager of a printing works is known as a printer even though he may never have printed a piece of type in his life. Whatever we may call the man who makes-ready and who is something of a mechanic in maintaining the machine which prints, let us remember his skill and craftsmanship upon which so much depends. A machine is only as good as the man who operates it.

the influence of sizing is to make the valleys more difficult to reach. Hand-made papers are generally (but not always) rough and hard sized, and are so difficult to print on when dry that they are usually slightly damped to soften the surface and allow the ink to reach the bottom of the little valleys. Damping increases the tendency to thicken the strokes of the type.

Coated papers have a surface of china clay which means that the ink is not printed on paper at all but on china clay which can be given an extremely smooth, glossy surface. Such an intrinsically unpleasant paper was devised in order to print properly the minute dots of a half-tone block. These dots are only a few thousandths of an inch wide, and if there were valleys in the paper only a few thousandths of an inch across, it follows that some dots would fail to print and thus ruin the tone. China clay produces a surface smooth enough to print the finest dot as yet made on a half-tone block. Art paper, then, is an unfortunate necessity in order to print half-tone blocks. But type must often be printed on the same paper as the block, changing the appearance of the type considerably. On pages 24–25 a number of type faces are printed side by side on art paper and on book paper, demonstrating the influence the paper has on the appearance of the type face.

Broadly speaking, art paper has the effect of thinning down the type, sometimes to a mere ghost of its strength on antique. Only a few types retain any vigour on art paper, the best being Plantin 110, Times Roman, with Bembo a possible third. Modern-face types tend to dazzle more then ever on art paper and are best avoided for continuous reading. Long-continued reading in any type printed on art paper is tiresome, even hurtful, but it cannot always be avoided.

BROADSIDE

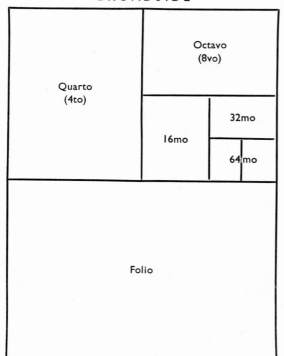

Here are a few Standard Sizes of Paper which the student is recommended to commit to memory:

CROWN 15″ × 20″
Untrimmed Quarto 10″ × 7½″, Octavo 7½″ × 5″

ROYAL 20″ × 25″
Untrimmed Quarto 12½″ × 10″, Octavo 10″ × 6¼″

DEMY 17½″ × 22½″
Untrimmed Quarto 11¼″ × 8¾″, Octavo 8¾″ × 5⅝″

MEDIUM 18″ × 23″
Untrimmed Quarto 11½″ × 9, Octavo 9″ × 5¾″

Fig. 23. Divisions of a sheet of paper.

International Standard Paper Sizes

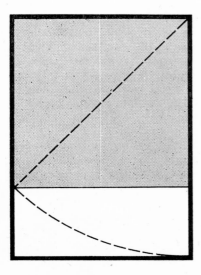

Basis of the international standard series is a sheet whose sides are in the ratio 1: √2— the 'Golden Square', as it is known to architects and designers. However many times the sheet is folded in halves, the subdivisions always have their sides in the same ratio, which greatly facilitates enlargement or reduction of printed matter, diagrams and drawings by photographic means.

Fig. 24. Standard Paper Proportion.

AN internationally standardised system of sizes for printing and writing papers has been in operation on the Continent for some thirty years. Many other countries throughout the world have adopted the system, which is referred to variously as DIN (Deutsche Industrie Normen) sizes, Continental Standards or, with partial accuracy, the 'A' series.

There are increasing signs of interest in international standard sizes among paper users and printers in Great Britain. Already the British Standards Institution has included two of the most commonly used sizes of the international 'A' series in its specifications relating to manufacturers' trade and technical literature, and a new British Standard specifying inter-national trimmed metric sizes of paper for both stationery and printed matter is in course of preparation.

Developments in European free trade are stimulating a wider interest in possible ways of integrating British and Continental trade practices and requirements more closely. As a result, adoption of international standards of paper sizes in Britain seems likely to be given a new momentum. With this in mind, we have outlined some characteristic features of the international system in a form which we hope readers will find both interesting and useful.

Supporters of the international system claim that its extension to this country would bring many economic advantages. In the long run, it is argued, fewer sizes must mean cheaper production costs. Fewer stocks would need to be carried by manufacturers and suppliers, with consequent savings in stock control and administration. Nor, judging by Continental experience would these economies necessarily involve sacrificing variety of product.

For stationery, a comprehensive matching of paper and envelope sizes is achievable within a notably reduced range of sizes. For print design, there seems ample flexibility in the various formats which are obtainable.

International standard sizes are based on the metric system. The basic sheet size of the 'A' series is one square metre in area, and therefore permits the direct use of the grams per square metre (gsm) method of designating paper substance.

TYPE faces may be regarded as a branch of lettering, for making printing type is but one of many methods of making letters. In themselves, letters have no meaning, they are phonograms, that is symbols representing the sounds of speech, and only convey ideas when arranged in the groups we call words.

But long before the alphabet was invented, people recorded ideas in a variety of ways, the most significant from our point of view in approaching type being the system of pictorial images known as pictograms. These, as the name suggests, are simplified pictures of the things or attributes to be recorded. Thus a drawing of an eye would represent the word eye or the notion of seeing. Pictograms are of necessity very limited in their range as they can only bring to mind those things or actions that are capable of being made into intelligible pictures; but it is not a great step to arbitrary shapes which it is agreed shall symbolize ideas. Thus grew up the system of ideograms which survives in China and Japan. In some Chinese characters the original pictogram is still discernable even to unimaginative Western eyes, but in most, the picture has long since been turned into abstract shapes that must be learnt by heart. Ideograms, though an evident improvement on pictograms, have the great advantage that a different character (or modification of an existing one) is required for each idea symbolized. While our children have but twenty-six shapes to learn/ from which every word in the language can be built up, Chinese children have some thousands to remember. A simplified version of Chinese which compares with Basic English has about 2,000 characters which will convey basic ideas, but a thousand or two more are needed to communicate with any subtlety.

The Egyptians, at least 3,000 B.C., had evolved a method of writing which included pictograms, and symbols representing letters and syllables. They were within a hair's breadth of inventing an efficient alphabet.

The origin of our alphabet, the Latin, is still somewhat obscure, but there is general agreement among scholars that the Latin derived from the Greek, which was also the parent of Cyrillic,

another of the most important alphabets of the world. The Greeks probably obtained their alphabet from the Phœnicians who in turn owe a lot to the Egyptians. Some of our letters can be traced without much serious dispute right back to the Egyptians. Our letter A turned upside down thus ɣ, only needs a couple of dots in the enclosed triangle to make the resemblance to the head of an ox unmistakable. The letter A was the first letter of the word Aleph, meaning an ox, which, together with Beth, meaning a house, survive through the corresponding Greek Alpha and Beta in our word alpha bet.

In order to see the resemblance between our capital A and an ox's head it was necessary to turn the letter upside down. This reversal of direction of letters has occurred many times in the history of letter forms owing to a variety of causes. But there are three main forces or influences that tend to modify the shapes of letters at all times and places. They are: (1) the tool or instrument the letter is made with; (2) the material the letter is made in or on; (3) the speed at which the letter is made. Letters made in a hurry are apt to tip over, and when it is understood that the direction of writing has changed from right to left to the present custom of left to right, it is not surprising to find that many of our familiar letters used to face the opposite way.

Early Greek inscriptions run alternately from left to right and then right to left. This is known as Boustrophedon script. By the beginning of the Christian era it was firmly established for Latin inscription to run from left to right, and we will now concern ourselves only with important landmarks in the evolution of the letter designs which you see as you read this book.

One of the most important periods is that of Rome in the early second century, and in that period the most famous example of lettering is that on the column erected to the glory of the Emperor Trajan about A.D. 114. This inscription is so well known, and a full-size cast of it may be seen at the Victoria and Albert Museum, that it seems unnecessary to describe it in detail. Suffice it to say that these noble letters have remained an inspiration to lettering craftsmen

FOUR MAIN STAGES IN THE

Development of the Alphabet

MEMORY SIGNS (*Mnemonics*)

Knot writing, notches in wood. Used by many primitive peoples, some even today.

PICTORIAL SIGNS (*Pictograms*)

Simplified pictorial representations of the things or ideas intended, as used by American Indians. Other examples occur in Egyptian hieroglyphics, Chinese, Japanese.

SIGNS FOR IDEAS (*Ideagrams*)

Often derived directly by simplification from pictograms, but arbitrary shapes were used to represent abstract ideas that cannot be shown in a picture. Employed largely in Chinese and Japanese.

SIGNS FOR SOUNDS OF SPEECH (*Phonograms*) *THE ALPHABET*

An alphabet is thus a series of arbitrary symbols representing the sounds of speech. The three most important alphabets in the world are the Latin, Cyrillic, and Arabic. The Latin and Cyrillic (the alphabet used for Russian, Bulgarian, etc.) are both derived from Greek, the Greek appear-ance remaining most strongly in Cyrillic. Arabic developed on different lines and has remained calligraphic in its forms where Latin, and to some extent Cyrillic, has achieved a formal architectural quality.

Fig. 25.

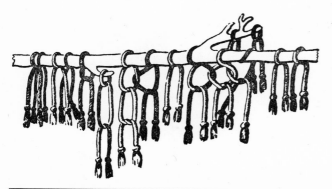

Mnemonic or memory signs

KNOT WRITING as used by the ancient Chinese, Persians, Mexicans and Peruvians. It is said that even today in Peru some shepherds know the language of knots.

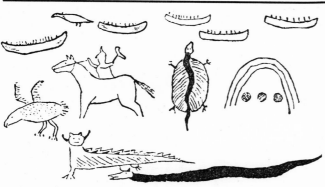

Pictograms

PICTURE WRITING. This is a picture letter found near Lake Superior, and means that the fifty-one men in the five canoes crossed the lake for an invasion lasting three days (indicated by the three suns under the arch of the sky). The turtle and the eagle mean that the invasion ended successfully.

Ideagrams

SIGNS FOR IDEAS. Here are a few typical ideagrams from Chinese and from everyday use.

Phonograms

SIGNS FOR SOUNDS. Generally the signs for sounds would be truly alphabetic, but the Egyptian hieroglyphics show an intermediate stage when language was recorded partly in phonograms and partly in ideagrams. Here is also a specimen of Cyrillic and Arabic, the other two most important alphabets in the world.

ever since. The fame of this inscription has been so great that some people are inclined to imagine that our printing types have evolved directly (as though from father to son) from this inscription. This is not true. There were many fine inscriptions during the same period, when a tradition of first-rate lettering and inscription-cutting flourished. There is little evidence that this particular inscription enjoyed in the past, the spotlight reputation it has had during the last fifty or sixty years.

What must be made clear to the beginner is that the beautiful letters which reached a peak of excellence during the reign of the Emperor Trajan were what we call capital letters, or in the technical language of palæographers, majuscules. What we call lower-case or small letters (minuscules) were evolved in the following few centuries.

We have said that there are three main influences which tend to modify the shapes of letters and all three obviously played a part in evolving the minuscule from the formal capitals of second-century Rome. Imagine the clean triangular form of cap A being made on a wax-tablet with a stylus, which was the Roman equivalent of the modern scribbling pad and pencil. The points would soon get rounded and the hasty writer would not bother to lift his stylus to make the horizontal cross-stroke but take it diagonally upwards from the base of the stem. It is not difficult to understand how the shapes would again be modified through the development of writing with a chisel-edged reed or quill pen on vellum.

It is safe to say that the norm, the standard, the influence in lettering of the second century A.D. was the letter cut in stone—the inscriptional, monumental letter. The scribe, learning to use the broad-nibbed pen, took as his accepted shape, that of the capital letters familiar on the walls of buildings. By its very nature, the pen cannot readily make some shapes which are natural enough to the chisel or brush, and so we find, as we should expect, that the formal, pen-written capitals, while obviously derived from inscriptional lettering, were equally obviously different in some respects. The squareness of

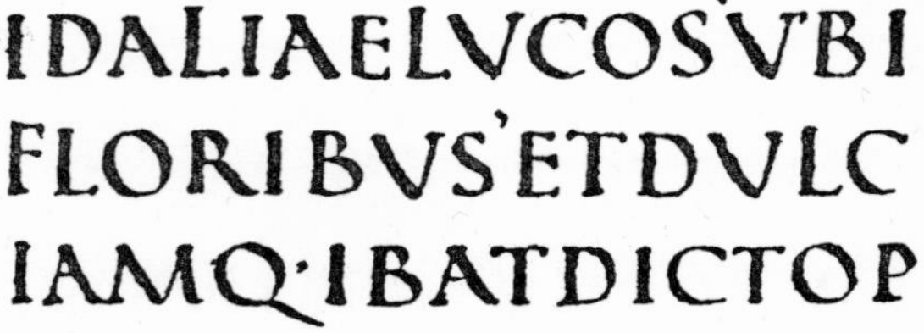

Fig. 26. Quadrata or Square Caps.

Fig. 27. Rustic Caps.

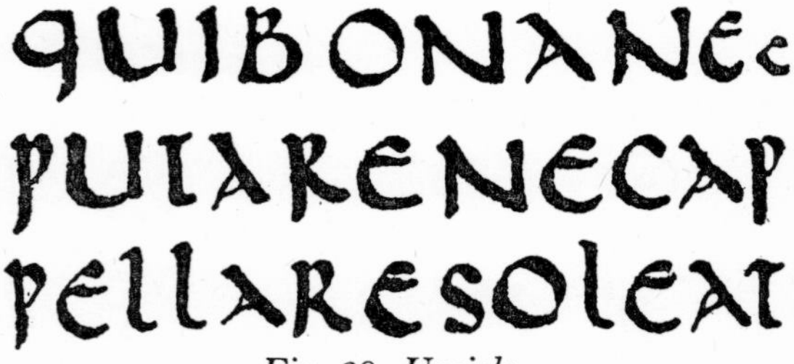

Fig. 28. Uncials.

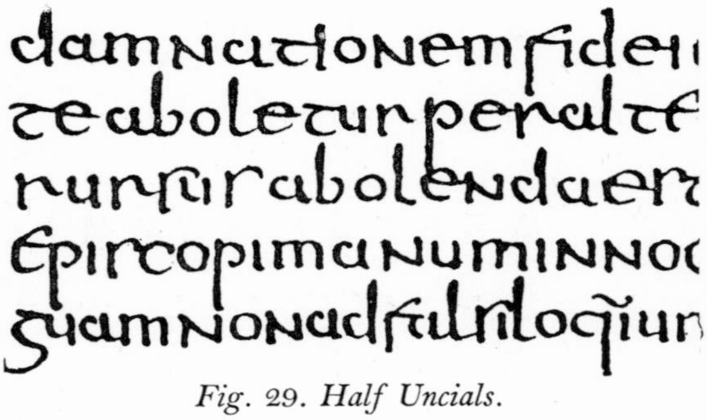

Fig. 29. Half Uncials.

many letters like E was retained. This style of writing which was practised perhaps from the second to the fifth century is known as Quadrata or Square Capital writing (Fig. 26).

There was also a compressed version known as Rustic Caps (Fig. 27).

Observe that all writings so far have been in capitals or majuscules. Another style of majuscule writing employed as a literary hand is known as Uncial. This is a 'modification of capitals in which curves are freely introduced as being more readily inscribed with the pen on soft material such as papyrus' or vellum. Compare the cap E or M in the Quadrata or Square Capitals with the Uncials and the rounded character of the uncial is very noticeable. These noble letters were used from the fifth to the eighth century for the finest books. Notice also that parts of some letters begin to project above and below the two parallel lines which form the top and bottom boundary of capital letters and which we have agreed to call the cap line and base line. These ascenders and descenders, as they are called, grow even more pronounced in the style of writing known as Half Uncial. Even an untrained eye will see the resemblance to our familiar lower-case, in fact, it may appear to some people to be a mixture of caps and lower-case. This is what actually happened. The uncials were formal, imposing, and not very quickly written. The ascending and descending letters, developed in the cursive form for ease and quickness in writing, were mixed with uncials, though not in the way we employ capitals with lower-case. Roman half uncials may be regarded as marking the change from majuscules to minuscules, or, in everyday language, from capitals to small letters.

The development of a freely and quickly written minuscule was a most important step in the evolution of the letter forms we now read.

In the history of our letter forms, the names of the Emperor Charlemagne and the Anglo-Saxon churchman and scholar, Alcuin of York are prominent. It was at the invitation of Charlemagne that Alcuin took charge of the Abbey of St. Martin at Tours, with the task of correcting the Bible 'to secure conformity in future copies

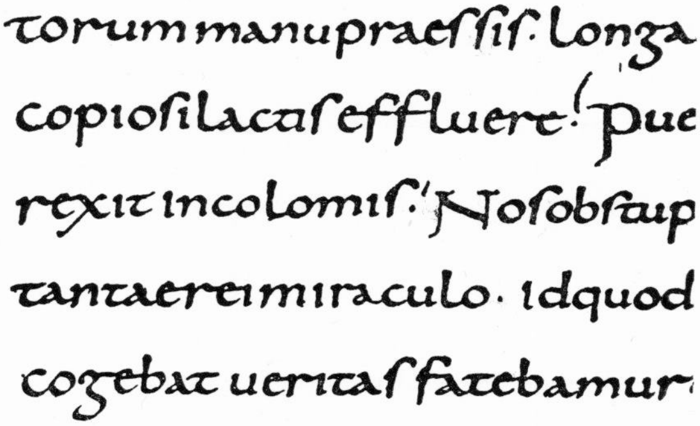

Fig. 30. *Caroline Minuscules.*

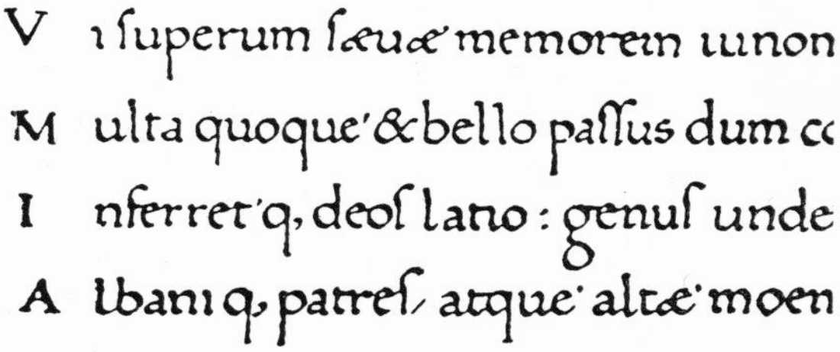

Fig. 31. *Italian 15th. century writing.*

of the sacred text,' and to revise the order and canon of the Mass. A very large amount of writing was done, and under the supervision of Alcuin a form of handwriting was evolved which was simple, beautiful and economic of space. This script became the parent of the letters in which this book is printed. It became known as the Caroline Minuscule and remained the dominating book-hand in Europe for centuries. It should be noted that the improvement in lettering was associated with the movement to improve the text, in other words, developments in the craft of writing or lettering are usually associated with literary or cultural movements.

That is true of the next important landmark which is in the fifteenth century, the time of the great Renaissance. As Stanley Morison has pointed out, 'By the time printing was invented, handwriting was almost in need of another revision.' The scribes, copying the recently discovered classical texts, also copied the handwriting in which the texts were written. As a large number of these scripts were Caroline, a 'neo-Caroline' hand grew up.

The humanists applied themselves enthusiastically to the cultivation of fine handwriting as they

*Fig. 32. Spanish Humanistic
handwriting.*

did to the study of classic and pre-Christian literature. The fashion for classical antiquities in fifteenth-century Italy might be likened to the fashion for Gothic in Victorian England. The handwriting in which the works of antique authors were found became known as the *littera antiqua* (antique letter), and was the accepted hand for secular manuscripts. The pointed, angular writing was despised by the classical scholars and was called by them gothic or *barbarous*, a name which has stuck to that style of writing as to the architecture, so that its original significance is now lost in our admiration for Gothic culture.

Thus at the time printing from movable types was invented (almost certainly by Gutenberg, about 1440) there was a tradition of fine writing in existence in Italy, and at first printers copied this handwriting as closely as the different tools and technique would allow.

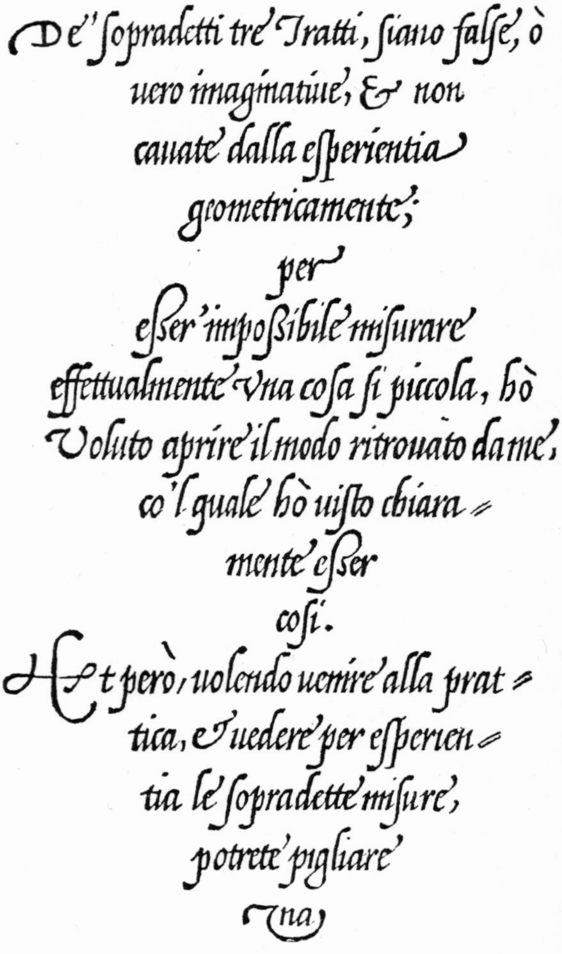

*Fig. 33. A page from Palatino's writing book.
Italian 16th. century.*

The Invention of Printing from Movable Types

STUDENTS are often perplexed by the varying dates for the invention of printing given in different books. To use a now hackneyed but still true expression—it depends on what you mean by printing. If a rubbing from a stone or metal inscription is a print (made with a pigment transferred by means of pressure) then printing goes back thousands of years to China. Stones and plates were cut with the deliberate intention of taking rubbings from them, and so served the same purpose as printing—namely to make identical copies of an original text. But rubbings are not generally regarded as prints.

A print is usually thought of as an impression on paper or other substance made by exerting pressure on the back of the paper while it is in contact with an inked surface. The inked surface may be a block of wood, a copper plate or a slab of stone. In this sense printing again goes back to China in the ninth century A.D. The oldest printed book is the Diamond Sutra, a Sanskrit holy book printed from woodcuts, and is dated 868. This book contains both illustrations and text cut on the same wood-blocks. These were inked and then the image transferred to paper by means of pressure on the back. This is certainly printing, but it is not printing from movable types which was the important invention of fifteenth-century Europe. By the Chinese method each page required a completely new block to be cut for it, and it alone. The blocks cut would be no use for any other book. In a language like Chinese where a different character is required for almost every word, there was not much to be gained by separate letters that could be distributed and used again. At least, in the past, when all type was set by hand, the labour of cutting a fresh block for each job hardly exceeded the labour of casting separate characters, setting them up and distributing them again. There is evidence that a method of casting numbers of identical types for setting, printing, distributing and resetting as required, was tried in China centuries before the invention in Europe, but it was never developed, probably for the reason given above—that for the Chinese language and the methods and equipment then used, no great gain was likely. There is no evidence and not

much likelihood that the earlier experiments in China had any influence on the invention in Europe which can be regarded as quite independent.

In Europe the situation was different. European languages need only a few more characters than the 'twenty-six soldiers of lead'; and a method of making large numbers of identical types at an economic speed was a need waiting to be satisfied.

It is curious that an invention so far-reaching in its effect as the invention of printing from

Fig. 34. Typefounder. 16th. century.

movable types should have its birth so shrouded with mystery and doubt. No precise year can be given to its beginning, and the inventor's identity has been disputed. But from the facts and legends that exist the strongest evidence is that the inventor was Johann Gensfleisch zum Gutenberg of Mainz. From what evidence there is, much of it being records of lawsuits involving Gutenberg relating to the purchase of printing materials, experts have agreed that for the purpose of celebrating centenaries and the like, 1440 shall be regarded as the birth year of printing from movable types in Europe. Thus, in 1940, *The Times* brought out a special Printing Fifth Centenary number which, though war conditions limited its size severely, was up to its usual high standard of scholarship.

What was it that Gutenburg invented that furthered so dramatically the movement towards literacy in the masses which is still going on today? A printing press was known and used; so was stiff printing ink. His greatest contribution to mankind, apart from the superb craftsmanship of his book, is surely in the establishment of a satisfactory method of accurately casting large numbers of identical types at reasonable speed. This enabled a man to get together a sufficient fund (fount) of types to enable him to set up many pages of a book, to distribute the type after printing, and to use the same types again. Thus a comparitively simple mechanical invention brought into being a process by which even the poorest person may now possess the living thoughts of the world's greatest thinkers.

There is the 'Haarlem Legend' which claims the honour of inventing printing for Laurens

Fig. 36. Bookbinders, 16th. century.

Janszoon Coster of Haarlem about 1440. But the evidence is slender and nothing like as strong as that for Gutenberg, who, in 1438, incurred debts with a carpenter for work pertaining to printing. This is discussed in *The Times* Printing Number in 1940. Let us therefore leave historians to find evidence to prove beyond doubt the identity of the inventor of printing and in the meantime, let us accept the name of Gutenberg and the date of 1440. It is well worth while for the student to fix that date as firmly in his memory as 1066, which seems to be about the only date remembered with any certainty by the average English schoolchild. The date 1440 is important in world history as it marks the beginning of widespread literacy, hitherto undreamed of. It meant for the first time uniformity of texts. That is, every copy of an edition would be textually identical, whereas when books were copied by hand, nobody could be certain that all copies would be the same, because different scribes might make different mistakes—to the confusion of scholars in distant places.

Fig. 35. Printers, 16th. century.

Type Follows the Pen

THE period between the invention of printing in 1440 and 1500 is known as the Incunabula Period and books printed during that time are called Incunabula. The word Incunabula is derived from a word signifying swaddling clothes, and the meaning has been transferred to the period of infancy in printing. It is a most interesting period when the revival of learning found a great ally in the new invention of printing. Many of the earliest printers were themselves scholars who welcomed the means to multiply, at what was then a great speed, their beloved authors, both sacred and profane, Christian and pagan. They were the publishers and typefounders, too. It was not for many years to come that the crafts and trades of typefounder, printer, publisher and bookseller were to be separated.

It was for the most part, then, cultured men who first took up printing, performing many of the operations themselves and certainly supervising the labour of less knowledgeable but manually skilled artisans. When making type they took for their models the normal handwriting of their own age and country. In consequence we find that Gutenberg's type closely resembles the current handwriting, which was Gothic at that time in Germany. There was a deliberate attempt to make the printed page resemble a manuscript as far as possible. It is scarcely too much to say that the early printer hoped that their works would be mistaken for manuscripts. The unwisdom of trying to imitate in one medium the productions of another, and the further unwisdom of trying to make a machine-made product look like hand-made, luckily did not survive. But for a time some men of culture were opposed to the mechanical production of books and the famous Duke of Urbino refused to have a printed book in his library.

The resemblance to manuscript was made even closer by the fact that originally, the text only, was printed and space was left for the large decorative initial letters to be added by hand. Frequently a tiny letter was printed in the space as a guide to the rubricator, as the man was called who painted these initials. In many existing books these tiny letters are all that is to be seen in the large white space at the beginning of chapters when the owner failed to have the colouring added by hand.

It was this adding of initial letters that provided employment for some of the scribes whose living had been taken away by the invention of printing. In some towns the scribes, who were organized in guilds, were powerful enough to prevent the setting up of printing presses for many years. But eventually printing prevailed, as was inevitable, and the attitude of mind towards the art changed. It was recognized as having beauties in its own right apart from those it took over from hand-work. The forms of the letters were at first copied from the scribes as closely as the technique of punch-cutting would allow. But soon the engravers who cut the punches began to modify the shapes until forms were arrived at more appropriate to printing than the calligraphy of the scribes. At first even connected letters (ligatures) were imitated in type so that the printer had many more characters than the twenty-six letters of the alphabet. These too, were eventually abandoned, with the exception of fi, ffi, fl and ffl, and one or two others which are still in use.

As we have said, there was a great enthusiasm during the fifteenth century in Italy for the newly discovered classic authors and a 'neo-Caroline' hand developed from imitating the script in which those authors were written. So before long we find in Italy types based on this *littera antiqua* (sometimes called 'white' letter to distinguish it from 'black' letter or Gothic). Another name often employed for the Roman as distinct from the Gothic style is 'humanistic', so called because the classical scholars responsible for the revival of learning and the resuscitation of handwriting were known as Humanists. This helps to explain some of the names that have been used to describe the various styles of types whose designs fall somewhere in between the true Gothic which is rigid, angular, without curves, and the Roman which has a generous proportion of curves. The rigid angular letter of Gutenberg (page 42) has been called textura, which name is applied to other types having similar characteristics. Some types,

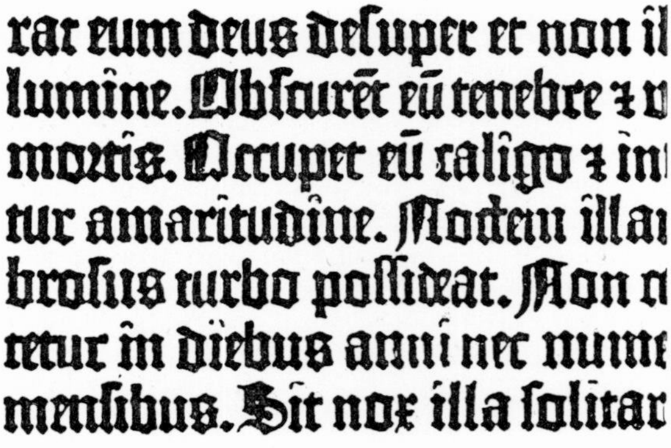

Fig. 37. Gutenberg's type.

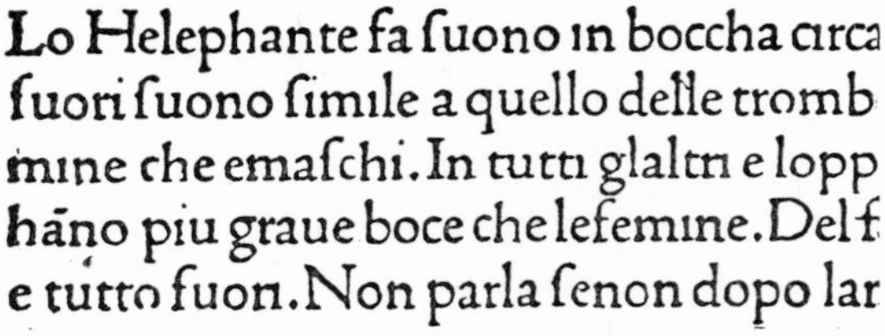

Fig. 38. Jenson's Roman Letter.

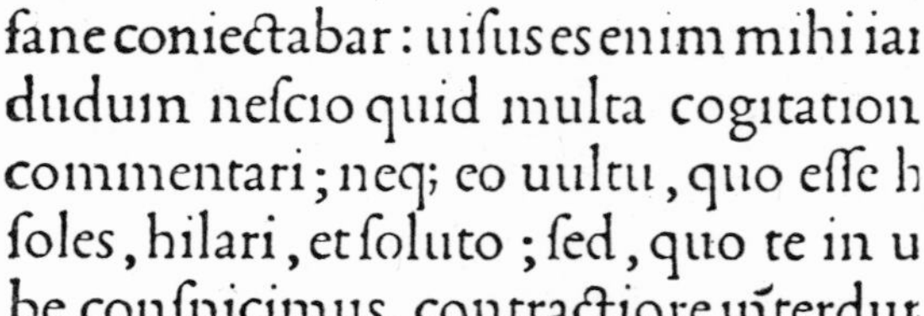

Fig. 39. Aldus's Roman Letter.

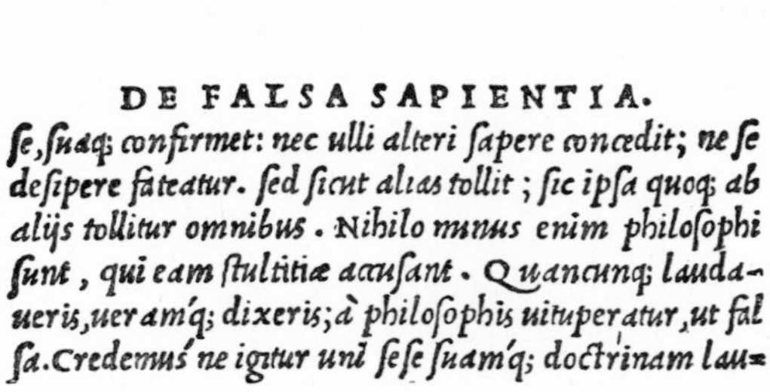

DE FALSA SAPIENTIA.

se, suáq; confirmet: nec ulli alteri sapere concedit; ne se desipere fateatur. sed sicut alias tollit ; sic ipsa quoq; ab alijs tollitur omnibus . Nihilo minus enim philosophi sunt , qui eam stultitiæ accusant . Quancunq; lauda- ueris, ueram'q; dixeris; à philosophis uituperatur, ut fal sa. Credemus ne igitur uni sese suam'q; doctrinam lau=

Fig. 40. The first italic type. Aldus 1501.

while resembling Gothic in many respects and yet having curves and other characteristics of roman, are called Fere humanistica, Rotunda, Semi-Gothic. Some authors give those names to separate groups of types which the student can follow up for himself. But as gothic type is not in general use today, and as Gothic is unlikely to be an 'influence' in the design of contemporary book types, we will confine ourselves to the roman letter which is gaining ground rather than losing it. For example, even in Germany, roman was gradually taking the place of gothic (Fraktur) until Hitler checked the tendency, and in Turkey the whole language has been adapted to the Latin alphabet, where it was previously in Arabic.

One Humanistic influence took hold of types in Italy, the Gothic style became more and more confined to ecclesiastical books, the roman being used for the secular and classical literature. With fine calligraphic models on which to base their types, and with a living tradition of highly skilled engraving and lettering, it is not sur- prising to find in Italy before 1500 some of the loveliest and most readable types that have ever been made.

Of these fine types the most famous are those of Nicholas Jenson and Aldus Manutius, both printers in Venice towards the end of the fifteenth century. Jenson's letter (1470) to be seen on this page, is a round, open letter, fairly strong in colour, stately and formal. Many derivatives of his roman types have been made, but none are better than the original which, unfortunately, hardly ever enjoyed the good press-work it deserved. Note the sloping cross-stroke to lower-case e; observe the wide H and the serifs on cap M which project at the top on *both* sides of the vertical strokes. Of this type Stanley Morison writes, 'No praise seems too high for it.' William Morris has copied it, so has Emery Walker, Cobden Sanderson and Bruce Rogers.

Rather late in the century, Aldus in 1495 brought out a tract by Cardinal Bembo in a type which is the ancestor of the large and important group of types known as old-face. It is much lighter in weight than Jenson's, the thin strokes are thinner in proportion to the thick strokes, the serifs are bracketed, the cross-stroke of lower-case e is horizontal. Altogether this is one of the most admirable types that have ever been cast. From the Aldine types it is easy to see the derivation of present-day types through the intermediate stages of Garamond and Caslon.

Even in so brief an outline of the history of type design one cannot omit to record that it was Aldus who introduced the kind of letter we know as italic. It was introduced for use, not as we do now for emphasis, but rather as a saver of space. Aldus brought out a series of pocket editions of the classics and devised italic type in order to get a greater number of words on to the page. It is regrettable that Aldus did not show the same good taste in italic that he had demonstrated with his roman letter, for his italic type (1501) has little to commend it when compared with Arrighi's lovely letter (1527).

Aldine types influenced the great French printers like Simon de Colines and Robert Estienne, and the famous Garamond (1545). These French types in their turn influenced Dutch letter designers—noticeably Christopher Van Dyck (1660). At this time Dutch types gained an international reputation, so that it became a way of commending a book to say that it was printed in Dutch letter. Not only was the influence of the design felt in England, but type itself was imported. In 1683, Moxon, the author of *Mechanic Exercises*, which treats of the craft of printing, refers to Dutch types in the following glowing terms:

> 'And for the commodious fatness they have beyond other letters, which easing the eyes in reading, renders them more legible; As also the true placing their Fats and Leans, with the sweet driving them into one another, and indeed all the accomplishment that can render Letter regular and beautiful, do more visably appear in them than in any Letters by any other People; And therefore I think we may account the rules they were made by, to be rules of true shaped letter.'

It was evidently these Dutch types which the famous Caslon used as a model. William Caslon I cut his ubiquitous Old Face between 1720 and

V os per inacceſſas rupes, et inhoſpita euntem
S axa Deæ regite, ac ſecretum oſtendite callem
V os huius ludi imprimis meminiſſe neceſſe eſt
V os primæ ſtudia hæc Italis monſtraſtis in o

Fig. 41. *Arrighi's Italic.*

IVuencus presbyter,natione Hi-
ſpanus,vir nobilis atque doctiſſi
mus,philoſophus,rhetor,poeta,&
theologus inſignis , & non minus
conuerſatione quàm ſcientia ſcri-
pturarum Eccleſiæ venerabilis, æ-

Fig. 42. *Garamond's variant of the Aldine Roman.*

Tardius aliquanto moleſtiuſque cum
G I O acta res eſt. Is enim recua ſcripſera
landis , Zelandiſque atque Burgundis
ctum deſignaret quando ſe hiſce prefec
h i j k l m n o p q ſ s t v u w A B C D E I
A B C D E F G H I K L M N O P Q S T V U

Fig. 43. *Dutch version of the Aldine Roman by Christopher Van Dyck.*

This is Caslon Old Face which was designed at a time when printing was done on a hand-press on damp hand-made paper. Caslon looks its best when conditions are near those for which it was designed.

Fig. 44. *Caslon's Old Face.*

Tibi autem porro ut non fit fu
Nam deteriores fumus omnes
Quodcunque inciderit in men
Putabit, pravumne an rectun

Fig. 45. Baskerville's transitional letter.

ottimamente fatte. Che però la
zia della scrittura forse più che i
tro sta in certa disinvoltura di ti
franchi, risoluti, spediti, e nond

Fig. 46. Bodoni's Roman letter.

I feel a childish tremor through me ru
Stronger than reason, lest by some fai
Fate's ear to our sad plaints should ye
And these our lives be thrown back or

Fig. 47. William Morris's 'Golden Type'.

By this the loue-sicke Queene began
For where they lay the shadow had
And Titan tired in the midday heate
With burning eye did hotly ouer-loo

Fig. 48. Doves type, 1901.

1726, and though there have been periods of neglect, it has been used and admired ever since. It was the first important type design to be produced in England, and remains one of the finest.

About the middle of the century, John Baskerville of Birmingham brought out a new type which differed in some respects from Caslon. The hairlines were thinner but not excessively thin, the distribution of weight in curved letters was rather more vertical than the typical old-face. Nevertheless, the serifs are inclined and bracketed, giving a general resemblance to old-face rather than modern. It is an open, comfortable type to read, with a distinct but not obtrusive individuality. At one time it was thought that Baskerville's letter had a direct influence on Bodoni, whose types brought to their logical conclusion those 'modern' tendencies which had been creeping in for some time. Nowadays scholars are agreed that Bodoni would probably have designed as he did if Baskerville had never been born. But Baskerville was an innovator in other things which were certainly copied on the continent. His wove paper and method of hot-pressing his papers to give a smooth surface were imitated and enabled the thin serifs of Bodoni to be printed adequately.

Bodoni, who was a printer in Parma in the late eighteenth century, produced a full-blooded modern type with the characteristic thin hairlines, fine unbracketed serifs and vertical stress in curved letters. These in their turn led to the 'fat-faces' which were so popular in posters in the early nineteenth century and which have had a revival in recent years.

Modern-face types remained popular, even for the main text of books, during most of the Victorian era. But the contribution of Victorian designers to the history of type was not in text types but in decorative and often fantastic display types. Many of these, too, are enjoying a revival, and there is a tendency for some artists to imitate Victorian title-pages with the titles and authors' names involved as part of the picture—the letters themselves often being stunted, contorted trees and the like.

After much shoddy typography came a great revival in the '90s. There was a general reaction, by many cultured people, against the ugliness of industrial England and the absence of aesthetic standards in the crafts. Prominent among the prophets crying in an artistic wilderness and striving to turn it into a paradise was William Morris. He founded his Kelmscott Press in order to produce the Book Beautiful. He found his inspiration in the fifteenth century and modelled his books on the general plan of the fifteenth-century Italian books. He imitated Jenson's type, though some people might regard it as a travesty. William Morris did many things and most of them he did well, and though no book designer today would use the heavy types, the closely-packed lines, the luxuriant borders of Kelmscott volumes, all respect the ideas for which Morris struggled and the vigour with which he fought.

Shortly after, Cobden Sanderson and Emery Walker set up the Doves Press with similar high ideals but produced books totally different in appearance. Morris's books teemed with decoration that almost literally spilled off the page; Emery Walker's trim tomes were as solemn as a judge, and the most ornament he would allow himself was an occasional coloured initial. Self-discipline was exercised to the point of asceticism. But the Doves severity was a good counterblast to the Kelmscott exuberance, and the two presses and their work mark the beginning of a typographic renaissance of which we are feeling the benefit today. Men are now trying to produce books for the many with something of the zeal and idealism with which William Morris, Cobden Sanderson and Emery Walker catered for a wealthy few.

In the twentieth century one of the most influential men in letter design was Edward Johnston, a calligrapher of genius, whose work, though small in quantity, bears comparison with the great scribes of the Middle Ages. Johnston's most influential *type* is the sanserif he designed for the Underground Railways—a letter so different from the medieval hands he loved to write. But it was Johnston the man and teacher, and his book *Writing and Illuminating and Lettering*, that had such a far-reaching effect. He made so many people care for and love good writing and lettering, that the ground was prepared for good craftsmanship and artistry when it appeared.

It was after the 1914-18 war that there came a big improvement in printing in England and when good types began to be available for general use. (Kelmscott types were of course private, and in any case had little commercial value, and the Doves type came to a tragic end in the Thames at Hammersmith.)

With Stanley Morison as typographic adviser, the Monotype Corporation began to put on the market well-cut revivals of old types selected with taste supported by considerable knowledge. Before the 1914-18 war there were only two or three good types available for printers—types like Caslon, Fry's Baskerville, which had to be hand-set, and Imprint, which had been cut for machine-setting just before the war. When the recent war started in 1939, that number had grown to at least twenty-five or more. A large number of these types are frankly revivals dug out of the past, but Perpetua and Gill Sans, designed by Eric Gill, are unquestionably as original as a type can be. Eric Gill has left his mark in the history of type.

Nothing has been said of America so far, because until recently America did not contribute anything of importance to type design. No outline of type history would now be complete without the name of Frederic Goudy who died in 1947, having produced over 100 different types. It is only to be expected that a considerable proportion of such a large output should prove ephemeral, but Kennerley, Goudy Modern, do not tarnish with time. One cannot but pay tribute to this G.O.M. of type who twice in his life lost all his possessions by fire, but like the Phœnix he rose undaunted from calamity and went on to create new letter forms.

Another name from America is that of Bruce Rogers who designed Centaur on the Jenson model, and in some opinions improved on the old letter. Elegant and unquestionably beautiful, it is perhaps too light in colour for very wide employment. See page 76 *et seq.*

This is 24 pt. GOUDY MODERN Type
abcdefghijklmnopqrs *abcdefghijklmnopqrs*

This is 24 pt. Goudy Bold Type
abcdefghijklmnop *abcdefghijklmnop*

This is 24 pt. GOUDY CATALOGUE
abcdefghijklmnopqr *abcdefghijklmnopqr*

This is 24 pt. Goudy Heavy Type abcdefghiklmnopqrs

Fig. 49. A few of Goudy's many types.

Fig. 50. Victorian wood letter, printed from the original wood.

A Method of Study

So far in this book we have discussed briefly general theoretical considerations of an approach to type with a few of the technical terms explained and a nomenclature given. It now remains to suggest a method of study of the type faces themselves in order to learn to recognize them and to appreciate their qualities.

Without doubt the quickest and best way of learning to recognize a type face is to draw it. We have all had the experience, when being asked to draw some familiar thing whose shape we thought we knew intimately, to find so little we could remember, and we did not even realize our ignorance, until asked to draw it. Thus the drawing revealed a lack of knowledge which could then be corrected. It is also evident to most people that making the merest scribble of the shape of a thing will help to impress it on the memory in a way that looking only would not. This is very true of types which often differ from one another so very subtly or slightly that the difference may go unobserved until comparative drawings are made.

If you can draw freehand—all the better. Copy carefully an alphabet of capitals, which as we said earlier in this book came before lower-case in the evolution of lettering, and you will thus acquire an intimate knowledge of the proportions of the parents of our letter forms.

If you are not an 'artist'—and too many students hinder their own progress by saying 'I am no artist,' and thereby prejudicing their own mind to failure before beginning—it is a good thing to trace. Tracing is not 'cheating'. Intelligent and careful tracing is a legitimate and time-honoured method of study, and even those who can and like to draw freehand will find tracing a great aid as a preliminary exercise.

The paper to use is known to the trade as bond, and is made up and sold by suppliers of artists' materials in 'layout' pads. This paper is transparent but comparatively tough, and takes pencil well. The pads are used for layout in all advertising agencies and layout departments. Layout pads may be bought in many sizes from about 10 × 7½ in. to 20 × 25 in., so buy the size that is most convenient to you. Working from this book you will not need any sheet to be more than 10 × 7½ in., but if you also use a larger pad for sketching, sheets can be folded down to size. Don't trace odd letters higgledy-piggledly on large sheets of paper, which will inevitably get crumpled. Train yourself to be neat and tidy from the start.

Use a hard pencil, cut to a very sharp point so that the precise shape of the letter, and not an approximation, may be recorded. It is good discipline, though not absolutely essential, to try to keep the line being traced as even in thickness (or fineness) as possible, going round the contours very carefully and making sure that the exact relation between thick and thin stroke is recorded. It is important to make sure that the correct thickness of stem in relation to height is suggested. The character of a type lies so much in the relative thickness of the stem, and it is so easy to make all stems a trifle too thin or a trifle too thick. Make an effort to observe and memorize any feature which is only to be found in the particular design being drawn.

Also pay great attention to the shape of the counters, noting the proportion of width to height. Generally speaking it is true to say that if you take care of the shape of the counters, the outside shapes will take care of themselves. Many lettering craftsmen observe that the eye seems to follow the contour of the inside enclosed shapes (counters) more than the outer contour. Certainly, concentration on the shapes of counters seems to improve one's lettering and appreciation of letter forms. It must never be forgotten that the areas of white paper enclosed by the drawn strokes of the letter are as much part of the letter as the strokes themselves. The background is an inevitable, indispensable and integral part of the letter, as every decorative designer knows when designing a pattern. Sometimes the spaces left seem more important than the strokes drawn. When you draw a circle you are just as much enclosing or defining an area as indicating a contour.

A very great aid to the study and appreciation of type forms is to cut a type. Not in metal, which would be too difficult, but in linoleum and in a large size. An old fragment of ordinary plain household linoleum (not oil-cloth) would do. Draw on it a sanserif letter about 3 or 4 inches high, choosing one like B, D or E which must be reversed from left to right in order to print correctly. The tools required are a V-tool and a gouge. Cut round the contour with a V-tool keeping your eye on that side of the V which is against the contour of what will be the printing surface. When cutting the outside contour of, say, cap E, after making one cut down the vertical side, start the cuts for the outside of the top and bottom arms *from* the cut already made, not the reverse, or there is a danger that the corner will break away. Cutting the inside right angle at the junction of the arm and the stem, it is best to stop just before the tool reaches the angle and lift the handle of the tool so that only the top of the cutting edge just reaches the angle. A bevel is thus preserved in the angle, and under-cutting of the printing surface avoided.

When the letter is completely outlined, the gouge can play its part by clearing away the background, leaving the letter standing in relief ready for proofing. If no press is available, quite good prints can be obtained by inking the surface with a roller and laying a piece of toilet paper (which is a tolerable substitute for the thin proofing papers one used to get) on the inked surface. On top of that place another piece of smooth strong paper (preferably manilla) and then rub with a spoon or other hard, rounded object, over the parts where the letter is, and a print will result. This will give you something of the 'feel' of type in a way unlikely from working on paper only.

At this point it is desirable to stress the importance of learning one type thoroughly before attempting to learn many. In the long run, you will learn many types more quickly by mastering one first and then adding to it, than by trying to grasp many at once. Experience with a very large number of students has shown that those who tried to learn many types before one was mastered were uncertain of any a year after commencing the study. If you master one type thoroughly so that you can recognize it with confidence without having to say, 'I think it is so-and-so, but it might be this or that,' you

will have a standard at the back of your mind with which you may compare other types. You will then find that having conquered one, a second quickly follows, so that you have two standards by which to test future observations. Two, soon becomes three and four, and after that it will be quite easy to memorize a type by noting in what respect it differs from those you already know.

After a reasonable repertoire has been acquired, only practice is necessary to maintain it. The differences between some types are so slight that if they are not constantly observed and compared they will be forgotten. Nobody can remember all type designs, even those that have been issued in this century, and what is more—who wants to? A large proportion of type designs are not worth remembering; and of some, the world would not merely be no poorer if they were destroyed, but would be positively richer for being rid of a little more ugliness which is liable to poison the taste of the novice.

It is claimed for the types displayed for study in this book that all are good in their way. There are others that some people may prefer, excluded for lack of space, though in some cases availability has been the deciding factor rather than preference. Some will probably remain in constant use for a long time while others are likely to have a vogue, die out, and be revived at some future date. The latter may include Playbill, Albertus and Chisel, which have a vigour and decorative quality which, when properly used, are excellent. But fashions in display change almost as quickly as fashions for women's hats, and so types such as these come and go. Some tend to endure through the centuries and it is sound, enduring letters that are best studied first so that the standard of lettering, unconsciously acquired, may be of the finest.

One can scarcely do better than start on Perpetua. Perpetua is a twentieth-century creation and it is a sound educational principle to start with the known (the age in which we live) and work towards the unknown (in this case, the past). Perpetua was designed by Eric Gill, one of the best letterers of this or any age, and, for the student, this type has another virtue. Paradoxically, though it is a twentieth-century type, it is closer to the original Roman lettering of the second century than most of the other familiar types. Thus without being too antiquarian in outlook, while studying a modern type, the student will acquire a fine standard of proportions of letters in the spirit of the famous lettering on the Trajan Column. It was Gill himself who said, 'While we may remember Trajan lovingly in the museum, we must forget all about him in the workshop.' This supports the view that one should understand the past and then proceed to work in the spirit of one's own age.

After carefully tracing the contours of Perpetua capitals, do the same with the lower-case and finally the italic, remembering as you do so how lower-case evolved from caps, and then italic lower-case from roman lower-case. Don't forget that what we call italic caps are really sloped romans and are not different in shape from roman caps as are many letters of italic lower-case when compared with roman lower-case. Compare *A a* with A a. *A* is only a sloped version of A, but *a* is a different shape from a.

When all the shapes have been traced, try drawing one or two from memory. Then look for any features which strike you as interesting or characteristic and by which you might identify Perpetua. Study them, trace them, try to draw them from memory. See if you can 'spot' Perpetua in any book or advertisement. Note the general weight or colour which is important in identification as noting 'spot' letters.

At this point begin to study and trace another type. Caslon is recommended as being a well-tried, sound reputable type which is very different in some ways from Perpetua. Many laymen start by thinking that most book types look alike, but the differences grow with increasing study and familiarity. Then, after having traced Perpetua, the thin strokes in Caslon will seem astonishingly thin. Caslon cap E and F will seem wide. It is these differences that one should observe and note. Remember that Caslon was designed for printing on damp hand-made paper in a hand-press, when the hairlines would thicken appreciably. Caslon is a typical old-face or diagonal-stress type, and it is a good thing to

contrast it with a typical and obvious modern or vertical-stress type like Bodoni. The mechanical character of Bodoni will be very apparent after drawing Caslon. Bodoni might be rendered reasonably with ruler and compass. Not so Caslon, which is much subtler and has what artists might describe as more 'drawing' in it. The horizontal and vertical feeling of the vertical-stress types is very conspicuous in Bodoni and this constitutes a good norm for future reference.

The three types studied so far were all designed for books and represent only two (old-face and modern) of the four most important classes of type in general use. The other two groups are Sans Serif and Slab Serif. It is recommended that Gill Sans be traced next and memorized as the norm for sanserif letters. Gill Sans is perhaps the best of the sans types available for everybody to use. The sans type designed by Edward Johnston for the Underground Railway (now London Transport) is unquestionably first rate but is not available to printers, and this book includes only those types which are readily obtainable. Gill Sans is not 'monotone'. That is, all the strokes are not of uniform thickness but follow the traditional placing of thick and thin letters where a uniform thickness of stroke would result in a clumsy or conspicuous heaviness. The variation of thickness is only slight, but important.

Sanserif types enjoyed an almost phenomenal popularity between the two wars when controversy of a harmless kind was carried on as to the merits of sanserif letters. One school of thought ruled it out of serious consideration as 'ugly', 'unreadable', 'vulgar'. The other school regarded it as 'clear' and 'functional', free from unnecessary romantic accretions and as expressing the spirit of the 'realist' age that designed for use rather than ornament.

Sans types are still widely used, but the excited enthusiasms and antagonisms now seem a trifle exaggerated. It is difficult to imagine historians of the future regarding sans type as typical of this age as we regard Gothic writing as typical of the Middle Ages. On the other hand, we do not see any reason to get excited the about alleged ugliness of sans letters when well designed and used appropriately. But it is a leavening thought to remember that the earliest Latin inscription known was in sanserif letter. Nevertheless, for sheer beauty, the true Roman letter can hardly be bettered.

The method of tracing the contours might now be continued with a slab-serif letter so that a norm may be acquired of all the main groups of types. Everything that has been said of old-face and modern types applies to slab-serif types—that is, observe the proportions, the 'weight', and any unique features.

The monotony of tracing letter after letter of the alphabet may be relieved at an early stage by constructing words or groups of words—that is, designing simple jobs in the letter being studied. This combining of letters into words is very important as the eye must become sensitive to minute variations of weight and spacing. A type cannot really be judged piecemeal by examining letters separately only. All the letters must combine well in use, and it is essential to train your eye not only to be critical of individual letters but of the effect as a whole when letters are arranged in words.

The kind of simple job you might try at first is a nameplate such as you might put on an office door. Letter your own name in Perpetua, placing it carefully in a rectangle of proportions appropriate to the length of your own name. The size of the letter in relation to the total size of the rectangle must be considered and also the size of the margins.

A typographic book-jacket is another suitable job to tackle as it does not include many words to weary the beginner with much lettering, and yet the possibilities of striking effects are encouraging. It is worth drawing these first few layouts very carefully so that at first sight the design might be mistaken for the print. In this way your eye will become intimately acquainted with the shapes of the types and with the importance of careful spacing. Spacing modifies the appearance of a type very considerably.

It must be clearly understood that mastery of a subject depends not only on the method but on the frequency, duration and enthusiasm with which it is applied. In order to recognize types at sight they must be constantly observed in order to keep the minute differences fresh in your mind. This means frequent consulting of type specimen books. From time to time compare a particular letter of the alphabet as it appears in different types. For example, take lower-case a and compare it in Baskerville with Bembo, Caslon, Garamond, Bodoni, Bell, etc.

Finally, supplement this practice with the study of type history and such critical commentary as may be found in books and periodicals. Some recommended books and periodicals are given in the following pages.

BRASS RULE:
PLAIN,
DOTTED,
AND
WAVED.

Bibliography

Books on typography and its related arts and crafts may be divided into many categories, but attention is here drawn to the kind of book which is mainly a collection of reproductions of printed pages or illustrations, with little or no commentary, and that kind which is largely in words, with little or no illustration. Both kinds are valuable. Broadly speaking, knowledge once acquired and practised is acquired for good, and books which give only technical knowledge of the craft tend to be consulted less and less as time goes on. On the other hand, collections of first-rate examples of typographic design remain an inspiration and a pleasure even to the expert. Where the student can afford to buy for himself some of these books he will rarely regret purchasing those which are largely illustrations of fine typographical design. At the same time, a full understanding of type and its use cannot be acquired without considerable reading, and on the next page is a list, with commentary, of some of the best books I have read or consulted.

Many of these books are, of course, out of print, but a large number of them will be found in any large public library and some of them will be accessible in small libraries. There are few important standard works which cannot be obtained from the Central Library for Students which operates through the local public libraries, any of which will obtain on request nearly all the books mentioned here.

Book-borrowing is inevitable for most people. Students were ever an impecunious race, but the possession of books is a stimulus to study as well as an ever-ready source of reference. I personally distinguish between books to be borrowed and books to be bought. If you have little money borrow the books which give you elementary information which once acquired is likely to stick, and buy those books which are likely to be interesting or informative in years to come. In other words, buy reference books even though they may be a 'bit over your head' at present. Books of examples of good typography such as *The Art of the Printer*, by Stanley Morison, *The Nonesuch Century* and *Modern Book Production* are a prennial source of inspiration and delight.

Printing Types: Their History, Forms and Use, by D. B. Updike (2nd Edition. Humphrey Milford, 1937.) Well produced. A standard work on type history, with admirable chapters on typefounding, the history of the alphabet, etc. Written in good English style, it is very readable, though in its nature it is a book to be referred to rather than read from cover to cover. Some information has come to light since it was published which makes one or two items out of date, but it is not likely to be superseded as a standard work for a long time. Copiously illustrated.

Type Designs of the Past and Present, by Stanley Morison. (The Fleuron, 1926.) This book in 66 pages gives perhaps the best brief history of our types in existence. In unimpeachable prose supported by vast scholarship this book ought to be in the home of every student of type. Adequately illustrated.

Writing, Illuminating and Lettering, by Edward Johnston. (Pitman.) (Numerous Editions.) This book by the greatest English scribe since the Middle Ages might be called the letterer's bible. Indispensable to the student of letter forms.

Handbook of Greek and Latin Palæography, by Edward Maunde Thompson. (Kegan Paul, 1893.) This is still a standard work on palæography, tracing with numerous illustrations and a scholarly text the development of handwriting in Greek and Latin from the earliest times until after the invention of printing.

An Illustrated History of Writing and Lettering, by Jan Tschichold. (Zwemmer, London, 1946.) A good, brief, well-illustrated history.

Type for Print, by David Thomas. (Joseph Whittaker, 1936.) A short, beginners' book explaining briefly the technicalities of type.

Type Designs: Their History and Development, by A. F. Johnson. (Grafton & Co., 1934.) This book stands halfway between Updike and Morison's small book. While it is a reference book, it is not too long nor too 'difficult' to read right through. Amply illustrated.

Typographical Printing Surfaces, by Legros & Grant. This (physically as well as intellectually) weighty tome gives perhaps the most complete description of typefounding and its machinery known at the time of its publication, and much is of interest only to a few, but the chapters on legibility and the classification of type designs should not be missed by the serious student.

First Principles of Typography, by Stanley Morison. (Cambridge University Press, 1936.) A sober statement of the principles which should guide every typographer. Unillustrated.

An Essay on Typography, by Eric Gill (2nd Edition. Sheed & Ward, 1936.) As erratic, and occasionally as irrelevant, as much of Gill's writing, but it burns with a faith and an enthusiasm which, allied to Gill's genius as a lecturer, makes this a most stimulating book and an interesting contrast with Morison's sober statements. Some interesting illustrations.

Printing of Today. Edited by Oliver Simon and Julius Rodenberg. (Peter Davies, 1928.) Mainly illustrations of pages from books published in America and most European countries, including Russia. A delight and inspiration to lovers of typography and graphic art. Some illustrations are in colour.

The Art of the Printer. Editor, Stanley Morison. (Benn, 1925.) Only one page of text; the rest is 245 half-tone reproductions of pages from books 'composed in the roman letter printed from 1500 to 1900.' Gives a fair idea of what book pages looked like at different periods. Woodcuts, wood engravings and metal engravings are included on many pages.

One Hundred Title Pages, 1500–1800. Selected and annotated by A. F. Johnson. (The Bodley Head, 1928.) Well reproduced examples of the art of the title-page.

The Printing of Books, by Holbrook Jackson. (Cassell, 1938.) Valuable essays by an author of distinction with fine typographical taste.

The Art of the Book, by Bernard Newdigate. (The Studio, 1938.) An essay by one of our most distinguished book designers with a large number of illustrations of good examples of book design from type to wrappers.

Encyclopaedia of Type Faces, by Berry and Johnson and Jaspert (Blandford Press.) Perhaps the most complete and certainly the best collection of type-faces.

Modern Book Production. (The Studio, 1928.) Mainly reproductions, some in colour, of interesting pages from books published in Europe and America.

The Practice of Typography: A Treatise on Title-pages, by T. L. de Vinne. (The Century Co., New York, 1914.) Very interesting and well illustrated.

The Typography of Newspaper Advertisements, by Francis Meynell. (Ernest Benn Ltd., 1929.) An admirable essay followed by extremely useful tables for 'casting off', and a number of reproductions of advertisements selected with discrimination.

Authors' and Printers' Dictionary, by F. Howard Collins. (Oxford University Press.) An indispensable handbook of printing practice dealing with such matters as punctuation, alternative spelling, etc.

Rules for Compositors and Readers at the Oxford University Press. Humphrey Milford. A safe guide through vexed problems of punctuation, capitalisation, etc.

Printing for Business, by Joseph Thorp. (Cape.) 'A manual of printing practice in non-technical idiom,' says the sub-title.

The Printed Book, by Harry Aldis (2nd Edition. Cambridge, 1947.) One of the best short histories of printing.

An Introduction to Typography, by Oliver Simon. (Faber & Faber, and also Penguin Books.) A sound guide to book typography which the student is advised thoroughly to digest.

Printing Design and Layout, by Vincent Steer. (Virtue, 1934.) A practical introduction to layout for advertising. Gives a large number of type specimens though only a few letters of each type are shown. There is an excellent chapter on 'casting off.'

The Nonesuch Century. (Nonesuch Press, 1936.) A volume containing specimen pages of the first hundred books published by the Nonesuch Press. Many of the specimens are on the same paper as the original book, which emphasises the importance of paper in the appearance of a printed page, and at the same time makes the *Nonesuch Century* a valuable source of inspiration to the book designer.

The Use of Type, by John R. Biggs (Blandford).

Five Hundred Years of Printing, by S. H. Steinberg (Penguin Books). The story of the relation between printing and civilisation.

The Practice of Typography: Correct Composition, by T. L. de Vinne. (The Century Co., New York, 1916.) A sound technical treatise.

PERIODICALS

Typographica. Edited by Herbert Spencer. Lund Humphries. Bi-annually.

TM (Typographische Monatsblätter). Monthly. Ed. Rudolf Hostettler. Zollikofer, St. Gallen, Switzerland.

Print. America's Graphic Design Magazine. Bi-monthly. 535 Fifth Avenue, New York.

British Printer. Monthly. Maclean-Hunter Ltd.

Printing Review. Quarterly. 44–47 St. Martin's Lane, London W.C.2.

Archiv (Archives for printing, paper and kindred trades). Quarterly. Berlin.

PaGA (Printing and Graphic Arts). The Stinehour Press, Lunenburg, Vermont, U.S.A.

Print in Britain. Monthly. 97 Jermyn Street, London.

Book Design and Production. Quarterly. 110 Fleet Street, London. Strongly recommended to illustrators and typographers interested in book-work.

The Paper Maker. Hercules Powder Co. Ltd., 1 Great Cumberland Place, London, W.1.

British Printer. Caters mainly for the tradesman and is on the upgrade in its standard of design and scholarship.

Graphis. Published in Switzerland. Can be heartily recommended for the quality and range of its contents and for first-rate production. It is mainly composed of reproductions of posters, illustrations, advertisements, drawings, etchings, lithographs, etc., by good modern artists, balanced by shrewd selections from the past, which have ranged from Chinese stone engravings to eighteenth-century penmanship. The illustrations are accompanied by a short text in English, French and German.

The Monotype Recorder. Is a house organ issued by the Monotype Corporation but which has contained scholarly articles on type and type history besides helpful technical information. This periodical represents in itself a very high standard of commercial journalism and advertising.

Motif. A Journal of the visuals arts published three times a year by the Shenval Press. High aesthetic as well as technical standard of production.

COMPOSING STICKS, BODKINS, PLIERS, TURNSCREWS, SHEARS, Mallets, Planers, Shooting-sticks.

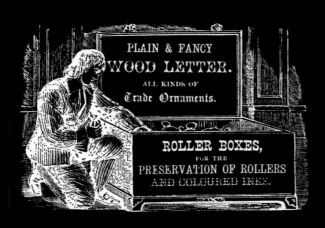

PLAIN & FANCY
WOOD LETTER.
ALL KINDS OF
Trade Ornaments.

ROLLER BOXES,
FOR THE
PRESERVATION OF ROLLERS
AND COLOURED INKS.

Type Specimens

As far as possible, all the normal characters of each fount are displayed in the largest size available so that the precise shape of each letter can be studied with ease. In some instances the type is not made above 48 pt. but even at that size, the shape is clear even to the untrained eye. After a complete alphabet of roman caps and lower-case, and italic lower-case (italic caps are virtually a sloped roman), a few letters of each other size are shown giving caps, lower-case and italic, and also small caps in the sizes where they are made—generally 14 pt. and smaller.

For the purpose of making layouts from these specimens, the base-line, mean-line and cap-line can be obtained for every size, so that even if a particular letter is not shown in the size required, the shape can be obtained from the complete alphabet in the largest size.

In such large families as Gill and Bodoni where there are many weights and widths of letter, only a few characters are given in the largest size, but the alphabet is continued in the smaller sizes, so that again a complete alphabet is generally shown. Where there is not a complete alphabet a little common sense will make it clear that the unseen letters can be deduced from the few that are shown. Thus E is sufficient to give you (near enough) F, L, T; G gives O and C, and so on.

From one point of view the ideal would be a complete synopsis of characters of every size, but that would make a book too clumsy to be good from a practical point of view. The arrangement of type specimens adopted in this book endeavours to give the maximum of information within the minimum space compatible with pleasant appearance.

Albertus

THIS is frankly a display letter and possesses a rich beauty. It belongs to that group of types in which the stems end in a swelling in lieu of a serif, and which is described as the Atlas group in Legros and Grant's book, *Typographical Printing Surfaces*. Designed by Berthold Wolpe, Albertus is based on a letter design used for an inscription on bronze.

The caps are undoubtedly better than the lower-case and are remarkable for the contrast in widths of letter typical of the Trajan tradition and so often lost in modern display types. The C, G, M, O, Q and W are wide; B and P are noticeably narrow; E, F, S are the classic half-square, but D, usually a wide letter, is narrower than the C. The S has a smaller counter at the bottom than the top, which sometimes makes it appear to be upside down to anybody brought up in the classic school where one is told that the upper curve of the S should be smaller than the lower. In the larger sizes, Albertus has an admirable monumental inscriptional quality that is a godsend to designers of dignified book jackets.

It has something of a hand-made appearance in some letters, particularly the lower-case a and g. The left-hand curve of the loop in g has flatness and angles which suggest bold, direct engraving on metal, as Rudolph Koch is reported to have done with Neuland type. There is a horizontal line on the upper part of the counter of the bowl of lower-case a which does not bear any relation to any other letter. On the other hand, the lower-case e looks comparatively sleek and machine made.

The Bold Titling in this series is also useful for book jackets, press advertisements and dignified jobbing printing of all kinds, where one or two words only are required in a bold yet dignified letter.

ALBERTUS: Series No. 481

ABCJ abcde 72 pt.

DEFGH fghijkl 60 pt.

IKLMN mnopqr 48 pt.

OPQRSTU stuvwxyz! 36 pt.

VWXYZ&£,;? abcdefghijklmn 24 pt.

TITLING: Series No. 324

RETHE

FAMILY &

AWAY FROM

ARISTOTLE AN

EMINENT SAGES!

BOLD TITLING: Series No. 538

WRITS 48 pt.

ARE FEW 36 pt.

GENERATION 24 pt.

HAS GIVEN THE 18 pt.

TRAJAN LETTER 14 pt.

ALBERTUS LIGHT: Series No. 534

ABCDEFGHIJKLM abcdefghijklmnopq 24 pt.

Baskerville

THIS most praiseworthy type is named after, and based on, the letter designed and cut by John Baskerville of Birmingham, about 1760. Recut by the Monotype Corporation in 1923. Baskerville was a most interesting person who tried many jobs before settling on printing; among them were writing-master and manufacturer of lacquer goods. Having turned printer-publisher (most printers were publishers at one time) Baskerville not only designed and cut his famous type, but invented the method of smoothing paper known as hot-pressing (hot-pressed paper). By pressing his sheets of paper, inevitably hand-made, between hot smooth plates, he obtained a smooth finish which enabled the fineness of his design to be satisfactorily reproduced on paper. This was admired and imitated on the continent notably by Giambattista Bodoni.

It is a wide-set type that publishers like when they have a manuscript which is rather short and which they wish to make occupy many pages. It is easy to read, normal in form, and can be used again and again for a wide variety of jobs without becoming tiresome and stale. The round, open appearance is easy to recognize, but there are some letters which will identify Baskerville without fail. Perhaps the easiest of these to remember are the lower-case g, the loop of which is open; the cap E, in which the lower arm projects further than the upper arm; the cap W, in which second and third stems meet at a pointed apex without the usual serif. Other 'spot' letters are cap C, where both arms end with fine barbs; flattened arch at the top of lower-case a and f which harmonise with the flattened curves at the foot of J and j.

Baskerville is appropriate for almost every book, and a large proportion of the miscellaneous ephemera evolved by advertisers. It is best leaded. The 10 and 11 pt. sizes are particularly useful for the average crown octavo book and for the text, as distinct from display lines, in press advertisements. Both sizes are improved by being cast on a 12 pt. body.

While the head serifs of lower-case letters like i, k, etc., are at an angle and all serifs are bracketed like an old face, the point of maximum stress in e is centrally placed like a modern face. Consequently it is known as a transitional face in between the thorough-going old-face and the out-and-out modern.

BASKERVILLE: Series No. 169

ABCDEFGH 72 pt.

IJKLMNOP

QRSTUVW

XYZ&£abc

defghijklmno

pqrstuvwxyzfi

1234567890!?

BASKERVILLE: Series No. 169

72 pt. *AEPQRSW&*

abcdefghijklm

nopqrstuvwxyz

60 pt. CAPS lower c *Itali*

48 pt. NOTE change *of the*

42 pt. WEIGHT between *sizes*

36 pt. THERE is a big jump *between*

30 pt. EIGHTEEN pt. & 24 pt. *Baskerville*

24 pt. THERE ARE many swash letters as *JTYZ*

18 pt. IN THIS FAMILY.   Here are a few more sorts *JQTYZ*

14 pt. THERE ARE ALSO some sizes like this which are cast *on the Didot point*

12D
13E SYSTEM WHICH IS USED ON THE Continent but may also *be obtained on English*

12D BODIES BUT VERY FEW PRINTERS stock these unusual sizes *More FGKPTUV*

BASKERVILLE: Series No. 169

HERE YOU SEE ELEVEN POINT C
lower case abcdefghijklmnopqrstuvwxyza

SMALL CAPS ABCDEFGHIJKLMNOPQRSTUVWXY
ITALIC CAPS Italic lower case abcdefghijklm 11 pt.

HERE YOU SEE TEN POINT CAPS ABC
lower case abcdefghijklmnopqrstuvwxyzabcd

SMALL CAPS ABCDEFGHIJKLMNOPQRSTUVWXYZA
ITALIC CAPS Italic lower case abcdefghijklmnop 10 pt.

HERE YOU SEE NINE POINT CAPS ABCDE
lower case abcdefghijklmnopqrstuvwxyzabcdefghi

SMALL CAPS ABCDEFGHIJKLMNOPQRSTUVWXYZABCDE
ITALIC CAPS Italic lower case abcdefghijklmnopqrstuv 9 pt.

HERE YOU SEE EIGHT POINT CAPS ABCDEFG
lower case abcdefghijklmnopqrstuvwxyzabcdefghijklm

SMALL CAPS ABCDEFGHIJKLMNOPQRSTUVWXYZABCDEFGHI
ITALIC CAPS Italic lower case abcdefghijklmnopqrstuvwxyz 8 pt.

12 pt. solid

The period between the invention of printing in 1440 and 1500 is known as the Incunabula Period and books printed during that time are called Incunabula. The word Incunabula is derived from a word signifying swaddling clothes, and the meaning has been transferred to the period of infancy in printing. It is a most interesting period when the revival of learning found a great ally in the new invention of printing. Many of the earliest printers were themselves scholars who welcomed the means to multiply, at what was then a

12 pt. (2 pt. leaded)

great speed, their beloved authors, both sacred and profane, Christian and pagan. They were the publishers and typefounders, too. It was not for many years to come that the crafts and trades of typefounder, printer, publisher and bookseller were to be separated. It was for the most part, then, cultured men who first took up printing, performing many of the operations themselves and certainly supervising the labour of less knowledgeable but manually skilled

10 pt. solid

artisans. When making type they took for their models the normal handwriting of their own age and country. In consequence we find that Gutenberg's type closely resembles the current handwriting, which was Gothic at that time in Germany. There was a deliberate attempt to make the printed page resemble a manuscript as far as possible. It is scarcely too

10 pt. (1 pt. leaded)

much to say that the early printer hoped that their works would be mistaken for manuscripts. The unwisdom of trying to imitate in one medium the productions of another, and the further unwisdom of trying to make a machine-made product look like hand-made, luckily did not survive. But for a time some

8 pt. solid

men of culture were opposed to the mechanical production of books and the famous Duke of Urbino refused to have a printed book in his library. The resemblance to manuscript was made even closer by the fact that originally, the text only, was printed and space was left for the large decorative initial letters to be added by hand. Frequently a tiny letter was printed in the space as a guide to the rubricator, as the man was called who painted these initials. In many existing books

8 pt. (1 pt. leaded)

these tiny letters are all that is to be seen in the large white space at the beginning of chapters when the owner failed to have the colouring added by hand. It was this adding of initial letters that provided employment for some of the scribes whose living had been taken away by the invention of printing. In some towns the scribes, who were organized in guilds, were powerful enough to prevent the setting up of printing presses

Bembo

MANY people regard Bembo as the most beautiful of the old-face designs and not without good reason. This type has poise. There is an effortless unobtrusive grace about it that brings finesse to a thoughtful layout and will retrieve from rank ugliness the most unconsidered of advertisements. It was cut in 1929 from a tract written by the humanist, scholar and poet, Pietro Bembo, and published by Aldus Manutius in 1495. The type was cut originally by Francesco Griffo who cut other types for Aldus, one of the great printer-publishers of all time. It has been suggested that this tract by Bembo might have been a typographical experiment, as the press-work (machining, as we now call it) was so clear and sharp, and far above the usual standard of the Aldine Press. The influence of this letter has been enormous. The French punch-cutters of the sixteenth century used it as a model. The Dutch followed the French, and our William Caslon based his famous type on Dutch letterforms. Hence old-face types may be traced to the original Bembo of 1495.

The present 'MONOTYPE' Bembo is one of the best book types available: being relatively condensed, it is a good space saver, and having long ascenders is legible and pleasant even when set solid. Though in general it must be described as a light type, it retains its character remarkably well on art paper. Large or display sizes as printers call them are very decorative and look admirable as initial letters or as headlines, and even on book jackets where reticence is required. Characteristics: The cap A has a sheared apex, K has a curved arm. The lower horizontal serif of E is longer than the upper. The inner stems of W cross over and are joined by a long horizontal serif.

BEMBO: Series No. 270

ABCDEFGHI 72 pt.
JKLMNOPQ
RSTUVWX:
YZ&ÆŒabcd
efghijklmnopq
rstuvwxyzfiffffi
1234567890!?

BEMBO: Series No. 270

60 pt. CAP & lower case

48 pt. CAPITALS & lower c

36 pt. CAPITALS lower c *Italic also*

ABCDEFGHIJKLMNOPQR STUVWXYZ&abcdefghijklmn opqrstuvwxyz No italic above 36

30 pt. CAPITALS & lower case *& Italic also*

24 pt. CAPITALS & lower case *and also Italic CAPS*

18 pt. CAPS ARE MAJUSCULES lower case letters *Italic lower case*

16 pt. CAPS ARE MAJUSCULES lower case letters are minuscules *Italic*

14 pt. CAPS ARE MAJUSCULES lower case letters are minuscules *ITALIC CAPS*

12 pt. CAPITAL LETTER SMALL CAPITALS lower case and the related *ITALIC and lower case*

11 pt. CAPS ARE MAJUSCULES lower case letters are minuscules *ITALIC CAPS and lower case*

10 pt. CAPS ARE MAJUSCULES lower case letters are minuscules 1234567890 *ITALIC CAPS and lower case*

8 pt. CAPS ARE MAJUSCULES and lower case letters are minuscules 1234567890 £ *ITALIC CAPITALS and lower case &*

6 pt. CAPS ARE MAJUSCULES and ower case etters are minuscules 1234567890£ *ITALIC CAPITALS and lower case &* ABCDEFGH

BEMBO: Series No. 270

12 pt. solid

for many years. But eventually printing prevailed, as was inevitable, and the attitude of mind towards the art changed. It was recognized as having beauties in its own right apart from those it took over from handwork. The forms of the letters were at first copied from the scribes as closely as the technique of punch-cutting would allow. But soon the engravers who cut the punches began to modify the shapes until forms were arrived at more appropriate to printing than the calligraphy of the scribes. At first even connected letters

12 pt. (1 pt. leaded)

(ligatures) were imitated in type so that the printer had many more characters than the twenty-six letters of the alphabet. These too, were eventually abandoned, with the exception of fi, ffi, fl and ffl, and one or two others which are still in use. As we have said, there was a great enthusiasm during the fifteenth century in Italy for the newly discovered classic authors and a 'neo-Caroline' hand developed from imitating the script in which those authors were written. So before long we find in Italy types based on this *littera antiqua*

12 pt. (2 pt. leaded)

(sometimes called 'white' letter to distinguish it from 'black' letter or Gothic). Another name often employed for the Roman as distinct from the Gothic style is 'humanistic', so called because the classical scholars responsible for the revival of learning and the resuscitation of handwriting were known as Humanists. This helps to explain some of the names that have been used to describe the various styles of types whose designs fall somewhere in between the true Gothic which is rigid, angular, without curves, and the Roman which

10 pt. solid

has a generous proportion of curves. The rigid angular letter of Gutenberg (page 42) has been called textura, which name is applied to other types having similar characteristics. Some types, while resembling Gothic in many respects and yet having curves and other characteristics of roman, are called Fere humanistica, Rotunda, Semi-Gothic. Some authors give those names to separate groups of types which

10 pt. (1 pt. leaded)

the student can follow up for himself. But as gothic type is not in general use today, and as Gothic is unlikely to be an 'influence' in the design of contemporary book types, we will confine ourselves to the roman letter which is gaining ground rather than losing it. For example, even in Germany, roman was gradually taking the place of gothic (Fraktur) until

8 pt. solid

Hitler checked the tendency, and in Turkey the whole language has been adapted to the Latin alphabet, where it was previously in Arabic. One Humanistic influence took hold of types in Italy, the Gothic style became more and more confined to ecclesiastical books, the roman being used for the secular and classical literature. With fine calligraphic models on which to base their types, and with a living tradition of highly skilled engraving and lettering, it is not surprising to find in Italy before 1500 some of the loveliest and most readable types that have ever been made.

8 pt. (1 pt. leaded)

Of these fine types the most famous are those of Nicholas Jenson and Aldus Manutius, both printers in Venice towards the end of the fifteenth century. Jenson's letter (1470) to be seen on this page, is a round, open letter, fairly strong in colour, stately and formal. Many derivatives of his roman types have been made, but none are better than the original which, unfortunately, hardly ever enjoyed the good press-work it deserved. Note the sloping cross-stroke to lower-case e; observe the wide H and the serifs on cap M which project

Bodoni

Bodoni is the most obvious of the modern face or vertical-stress types. It is based on types used by Giambattista Bodoni of Parma, in Italy, between 1790 and 1800, and cut in this version for use in contemporary printing in 1921. It has a geometric, mechanical, 'rule and compass' look with strong vertical emphasis and pronounced horizontal serifs. Every trace of calligraphy, so evident in the Venetian types, has disappeared. It is a *tour de force* of punch cutting, and if any outside influence is present it is that of the engraver on metal.

It is a narrow-set type, very noticeable in the cap C, G, Q, and in the O, which is far from being a circle. The inside lines of the counters of these 'round' letters appear to be parallel straight lines that turn abruptly into the hairlines. Cap A has a pointed apex, the C has a barb on both upper and lower arms. The vertical extension of the lower arm of G is very short; R has a double-curved tail in common with most moderns. The inner stems of W cross over, but not in the lower-case w.

Bodoni Bold No. 2 is virtually ordinary Bodoni with the stems thickened, the hairlines remaining practically unaltered in thickness. Bodoni Bold No. 2 should not be confused with Bodoni Bold, in which hairlines and serifs and stems are thickened. Ultra Bodoni is ordinary Bodoni with elephantine stems but with normal hair-lines. Letters like this were popular for publicity over a century ago and were known as Fat Faces. Not very legible, nevertheless Ultra Bodoni has a strength of colour and sparkle which has its uses in advertising. There is a type named Falstaff which is often mistaken for Ultra Bodoni and may be recognized by the curved brackets to the serifs noticeable at the foot of the left-hand stem of cap A, which is triangular in Ultra Bodoni.

Bodoni is not the best type for continuous reading, and if not well printed can be positively illegible, but its glitter finds favour with many advertisers and the various weights make it very useful for some of the multifarious functions of publicity. The thin hairlines make it unsuitable for photographing, either for line-blocks, photo-litho or photogravure.

BODONI: Series No. 135

ABCDEFGHI 72 pt.
JKLMNOPQ
RSTUVWXY
Z&£?!(ffi)0xl
abcdefghijkm
nopqrstuvwyz
123456789

BODONI: Series No. 135

72 pt. *ABCERSOW*

abcdefghikm

nopqrstuvxyz

60 pt. ABC abcde *Italic*

48 pt. KEATS poetry *shine*

42 pt. Byron burns with *passio*

36 pt. SHELLEY sings a *tuneful r*

30 pt. MILTON glows with a *lofty light*

24 pt. T. S. ELIOT speaks with an *authority a*

18 pt. REX WARNER spins a sonnet or a *thoughtful ode and*

14 pt. EDWARD LEAR jingles merrily his melodious *nonsense verses such as*

BODONI: Series No. 135

HERE YOU SEE TWELVE POINT
lower case abcdefghijklmnopqrstuvw
HERE YOU SEE TEN POINT CAPS ABCI
lower case abcdefghijklmnopqrstuvwxyzabcd
HERE YOU SEE EIGHT POINT CAPS ABCDEFGHI
lower case abcdefghijklmnopqrstuvwxyzabcdefghijklmn
HERE YOU SEE SIX POINT CAPS ABCDEFGHIJKLMNOPQR
lower case abcdefghijklmnopqrstuvwxyzabcdefghijklmnopqrstuvwx

SMALL CAPS ABCDEFGHIJKLMNOPQRST
ITALIC CAPS Italic lower case abcd 12 pt.
SMALL CAPS ABCDEFGHIJKLMNOPQRSTUVWXYZ
ITALIC CAPS Italic lower case abcdefghijklm 10 pt.
SMALL CAPS ABCDEFGHIJKLMNOPQRSTUVWXYZABCDEFGHI
ITALIC CAPS Italic lower case abcdefghijklmnopqrstuv 8 pt.
SMALL CAPS ABCDEFGHIJKLMNOPQRSTUVWXYZABCDEFGHIJKLMNOPQR
6 pt.

12 pt. solid

A question students frequently ask
of an instructor, or of themselves is
"How may I know a good type
when I see one?" This is a reasonable
question to ask and almost as difficult to answer as "How may I know
a good man when I see him?" The

12 pt. (1 pt. leaded)

A question students frequently ask
of an instructor, or of themselves is
"How may I know a good type
when I see one?" This is a reasonable
question to ask and almost as difficult to answer as "How may I know
a good man when I see him?" The

10 pt. solid

A question students frequently ask of an instructor, or of themselves, is "How may I
know a good type when I see one?" This is a
reasonable question to ask and almost as
difficult to answer as "How may I know a
good man when I see him?" The question
on type is easier, at least in this, that one
may get wider agreement as to what a type
is for, than the profounder and more con-

10 pt. (1 pt. leaded)

A question students frequently ask of an instructor, or of themselves, is "How may I
know a good type when I see one?" This is a
reasonable question to ask and almost as
difficult to answer as "How may I know a
good man when I see him?" The question
on type is easier, at least in this, that one
may get wider agreement as to what a type

8 pt. solid

A question students frequently ask of an instructor, or
of themselves, is "How may I know a good type when
I see one?" This is a reasonable question to ask and
almost as difficult to answer as "How may I know
a good man when I see him?" The question on type
is easier, at least in this, that one may get wider agreement as to what a type is for, than the profounder and
more controversial subject "What is mankind for?"
Once you are agreed as to what a thing is for, the
goodness or success of the thing will depend on whether
or not it fulfils the purpose for which it is intended.
What is type for? Obviously to read and to read with

8 pt. (1 pt. leaded)

A question student frequently ask of an instructor, or
of themselves, is "How may I know a good type when
I see one?" This is a reasonable question to ask and
almost as difficult to answer as "How may I know
a good man when I see him?" The question on type
is easier, at least in this, that one may get wider agreement as to what a type is for, than the profounder and
more controversial subject "What is mankind for?"
Once you are agreed as to what a thing is for, the
goodness or success of the thing will depend on whether
or not it fulfils the purpose for which it is intended.

6 pt. solid

A question students frequently ask of an instructor, or of themselves,
is "How may I know a good type when I see one?" This is a reasonable question to ask and almost as difficult to answer as "How may
I know a good man when I see him?" The question on type is easier,
at least in this, that one may get wider agreement as to what a type
is for, than the profounder and more controversial subject "What is
mankind for?" Once you are agreed as to what a thing is for, the
goodness or success of the thing will depend on whether or not it

6 pt. (1 pt. leaded)

A question students frequently ask of an instructor, or of themselves,
is "How may I know a good type when I see one?" This is a reasonable question to ask and almost as difficut to answer as "How may
I know a good man when I see one?" The question on type is easier,
at least in this, that one may get wider agreement as to what a type
is for, than the profounder and more controversial subject "What is
mankind for?" Once you are agreed as to what a thing is for, the

BODONI BOLD No. 2: Series No. 260

72 pt. **CAPS lowe*It***

60 pt. **THIN seri *thick***

48 pt. **GOawe*in***

42 pt. **JOYhopea**

36 pt. **LOVEonean**

30 **TONE *text* and**

24 **FORM colours *and***

18 **TEXTURE are *bi-product***

14 **GOOD printing is the *well and***

12 **PRINTING of what is *worth printin***

10 **ABCDEFGH abcdefghijklmn*ABCDEabcdefg***

BODONI BOLD: Series No. 195

60 pt. **THIS type has**

48 pt. **THICKER serifs**

42 pt. **THAN the**

36 pt. **ABOVE hea**

30 **NOTICE that**

24 **There is no italic**

18 **IN THIS Series No. 195**

ABsſ

ODmt

EFGfgh

HJKijkl

ULTRA BODONI: Series No. 120

LMN mno 36 pt.

NOPQpqrsti 30 pt.

RSTUM uvwxo 24 pt.

VWXMNyzab&ff!?£ 18 pt.

YZROPSTUabcdefghijkln 14 pt.

ABCDEFGHI kmopqrstuvwx 12 pt.

JKLMNOPQRST yzabcdefghijklmn 10 pt.

UVWXYZABCDEFGHIopqrstuvwxyzabcdefghijk 8 pt.

1 2 3 4 5 6 7 8 9 0

L. BEETHOVEN

ABCacw

DEFGdefg

HJKLBhijkls

MNOPTmnopr

BODONI BOLD CONDENSED: Series No. 529

QRSTUVqrstuvw 36 pt.

VWXYZAB vwxyzab 30 pt.

LENIN & STALIN yes no 24 pt.

HEGEL AND Schopenhauer Wh 18 pt.

WHITEHEAD AND HUME Einstein which 14 pt.

1 2 3 4 5 6 7

8 9 0 & £ (-)!?

Caslon Old Face

CASLON OLD FACE is one of the most consistently admired types to be produced in England. Designed and cut by William Caslon between 1720 and 1726, it achieved immediate success, and after a short period of eclipse it rose in favour once more, to remain a steady favourite among discriminating typographers.

Caslon was a gunsmith who became extremely clever and skilful in the engraving of gun-barrels. He was also very successful with the letters he cut for use by bookbinders, and was later persuaded by printers to give his attention to cutting punches for type. Again successful, he established himself as the first really competent engraver and caster of types in this country.

His first type was Arabic, to be followed a year or so later by his famous Old Face, whose homely, common-sense, comfortable look rapidly won for it a deserved popularity which halted the importation of Dutch types. Without any conspicuous features, it combines well in the mass. Ascenders and descenders are fairly long, which makes it appear small on the body. The 10 and 11 pt. seem very small, with the 12 pt. appearing to be much bigger and heavier than one would expect for only 1 pt. difference in body size. The 14 and 16 pt. are very beautiful and legible.

The cap A has a sheared, slightly cupped apex, with the main stem projecting slightly to the left of the thin stroke. The C has a barbed beak to both upper and lower arms. The cap E is wider than the classic E, and the lower arm projects further than the upper. The L also is wider than the classic. The lower-case a is fairly narrow and there is a flatness in the arch as it descends diagonally to a pear-shaped finial. There is a small sharp spur at the bottom of the stem of b. The head serifs of lower-case letters like b, d, h, i, j, k, l, m, n, p, r, and also the foot of u, are strong wedges. The link of the lower-case g lies horizontally along the base line.

Shapes of certain letters vary in different sizes, as is to be expected in a letter cut by hand, but in 42 pt., cap A, T, E, R, have differences that today we might think belonged to another series.

Caslon is a most versatile type which is equally at home in a Bible, a Balzac, or a booklet on ball-bearings. The larger sizes look handsome in display lines and the text sizes combine well into harmonious pages.

CASLON OLD FACE: Founders (Stephenson Blake)

ABCDEF

72 pt.

GHIKLM

NOPQRS

TUVJWX

YZ£&

1234567890

CASLON OLD FACE: Founders

72 pt. abcdefghijkl
mnopqrstuv
wxyzæfiflffi!

60 pt. CAPS lower ca
abcdefghijklm
nopqrstuvwxyz
ABDGMN

CASLON OLD FACE: Founders

CAPS lower & *Italics* 48 pt.

CAPS & lower case *italic* 42 pt.

CAPITALS lower case *Italics* 36 pt.

SOME SIZES are not so good *as others* 30 pt.

NEVERTHELESS this remains one *of the best* 24 pt.

TYPES EVER CUT Caslon Old Face derived *from the Dutch* 18 pt.

CAPITALS SMALL CAPITALS abcdefghijklmnopqrstu*abcdefghijkl*

ABCDEFGHI SMALL CAPITALS abcdefghijklmnopqrstuv*abcdefghijklmnopqrst* 14 pt.

ABCDEFGHIJ SMALL CAPITALS abcdefghijklmnopqrstuvwx*abcdefghijklmnopqrstuv* 12 pt.

HERE ARE TEN POINT CAPITALS ABCD
lower case abcdefghijklmnopqrstuvwxyz abcdefghij

SMALL CAPITALS ABCDEFGHIJKLMNOPQRSTUVWXYZ ABCD
ITALIC abcdefghijklmnopqrstuvwxyz abcdefghijklmno 10 pt.

HERE ARE EIGHT POINT CAPITALS ABCDEFGHIJKLM
lower case abcdefghijklmnopqrstuvwxyz abcdefghijklmnopqrstuvw

SMALL CAPITALS ABCDEFGHIJKLMNOPQRSTUVWXYZ ABCDEFGHI
ITALIC abcdefghijklmnopqrstuvwxyz abcdefghijklmnopqrstuv 8 pt.

HERE ARE SIX POINT CAPS ABCDEFGHIJKLMNOPQRSTUVWX
ower case abcdefghijklmnopqrstuvwxyz abcdefghijklmnopqrstuvwxyz ab

SMALL CAPITALS ABCDEFGHIJKLMNOPQRSTUVWXYZ ABCDEFGHIJKLMN
ITALIC abcdefghijklmnopqrstuvwxyz abcdefghijklmnopqrstuvwxyz abcdefgh 6 pt.

12 pt. solid

Properly to understand the question of the Point System, it is necessary to go back to the earlier days of the nineteenth century, when the type founders worked absolutely and implicitly to the orders of the printers. At that period the leading printers had their own standards for Pica, Long Primer, etc. They selected the face, or even had one engraved, to suit their own tastes and work. The type founders

12 pt. (1 pt. leaded)

Properly to understand the question of the Point System, it is necessary to go back to the earlier days of the nineteenth century, when the type founders worked absolutely and implicitly to the orders of the printers. At that period the leading printers had their own standards for Pica, Long Primer, etc. They selected the face, or even had one engraved, to suit their

Centaur

This elegant old style is a quiet-voiced, gentlemanly type produced on the 'MONOTYPE' in 1929 from drawings by the famous American book designer, Bruce Rogers. No type is completely original. Our ideas, like our bodies, have parents, though in the realm of invention there may be but one or a multitude of legitimate parents.

The parentage of Centaur can be identified without doubt. Bruce Rogers drew freely over enlargements of type from the books of Nicholas Jenson, the fifteenth-century Venetian printer. Bruce Rogers in his youth went to an art school and dabbled in the visual arts all his life, which was mainly spent designing for printing—mostly books. He thus brought a trained artist's eye to his long experience in printing. In drawing over Jenson's design he created something original while preserving some of the character of the Venetian types, just as a child may resemble both father and mother.

Centaur was used for the Oxford Lectern Bible published in 1935, which is perhaps the finest piece of book production of this century. It is small on the body and is therefore readable without leading. On the other hand it is light in colour, and without good black ink and adequate press-work it is apt to look grey and anæmic.

It can be recognized by its light weight and the vestiges of calligraphy in its forms, which were naturally more pronounced in the fifteenth-century types on which it is based, than after the development of the engraved modern. This is particularly noticeable in the terminal of the lower-case a. The arm of the bowl of cap R and D swings upwards before descending to meet the stem again, and the tail has a characteristic curve. The spurred serifs on the cross-bar of cap T are at an angle and are parallel. The stems of all letters are freely drawn and the second stroke of lower-case h swings round slightly instead of being quite vertical.

CENTAUR: Series No. 252

ABCDEFGH 72 pt.

IJKLMNOP

QRSTUVW

XYZ&£

abcdefghijklm

nopqrstuvwxyz

1234567890

CENTAUR: Series No. 252

60 pt. # CAPS & lower case

48 pt. # CAPITALS and lower c

42 pt. # CAPITALS and lower case

36 pt. CAPITALS lower case *also italic*

ABCDEFGHIJKLMNOPQRST

abcdefghijklmnopqrstuvwxyz & gg gy

30 pt. CAPITALS lower case and *ITALIC also*

24 pt. CAPITALS AND lower case also *ITALIC abcdef*

18 pt. CAPITALS AND lower case abcdefghijklm *ITALIC abcdefghijklm*

14 pt. CAPITALS SMALL CAPITALS lower case abcdefghijklmno *ITALIC abcdefghijklmno*

12 pt. CAPITALS SMALL CAPITALS lower case abcdefghijklmnopqrst *ITALIC abcdefghijklmnopqrst*

12 pt. solid

The period between the invention of printing in 1440 and 1500 is known as the Incunabula Period and books printed during that time are called Incunabula. The word Incunabula is derived from a word signifying swaddling clothes, and the meaning has been transferred to the period of infancy in printing. It is a most interesting period when

12 pt. (2 pt. leaded)

The period between the invention of printing in 1440 and 1500 is known as the Incunabula Period and books printed during that time are called Incunabula. The word Incunabula is derived from a word signifying swaddling clothes, and the meaning has been transferred to the period of infancy in printing. It is a most interesting period when

CENTAUR: Series No. 252

The period between the invention of printing in 1440 and 1500 is known as the Incunabula Period and books printed during that time are called Incunabula. The word Incunabula is derived from a word signifying swaddling clothes, and the meaning has been transferred to the period of infancy in printing. It is a most interesting period when the revival of learning found a great ally in the new invention of printing. Many of the

HERE YOU SEE ELEVEN POINT CAPS
lower case abcdefghijklmnopqrstuvwxyzfiffflffiffl

SMALL CAPS ABCDEFGHIJKLMNOPQRSTUVWXYZ
ITALIC CAPS and lower case ABCDEFGHabcdefgh 11 pt.

HERE YOU SEE TEN POINT CAPS ABCDEFG
lower case abcdefghijklmnopqrstuvwxyzfiffflffiffl 123

SMALL CAPS ABCDEFGHIJKLMNOPQRSTUVWXYZ ABCDE
ITALIC CAPS and lower case ABCDEFGHIJ abcdefghij 10 pt.

HERE YOU SEE EIGHT POINT ABCDEFGHIJKLM
lower case abcdefghijklmnopqrstuvwxyzfiffflffiffl 12345678

SMALL CAPS ABCDEFGHIJKLMNOPQRSTUVWXYZ ABCDEFGHIJ
ITALIC CAPS and lower case ABCDEFGHIJKL abcdefghijkl 8 pt.

HERE YOU SEE SIX POINT CAPS ABCDEFGHIJKLMNOPQRSTU
lower case letters are minuscules abcdefghijklmnopqrstvwxyz1234567890

SMALL CAPITALS ARE SHOWN IN THIS LINE ABCDEFGHIJKLMNOPQRSTUVWXYZ
ITALIC CAPS and lower case ABCDEFGHIJKLMNOPQRS abcdefghijklmnopqr 6 pt.

10 pt. solid

The period between the invention of printing in 1440 and 1500 is known as the Incunabula Period and books printed during that time are called Incunabula. The word Incunabula is derived from a word signifying swaddling clothes, and the meaning has been transferred to the period of infancy in printing. It is a most interesting period when the

10 pt. (1 pt. leaded)

The period between the invention of printing in 1440 and 1500 is known as the Incunabula Period and books printed during that time are called Incunabula. The word Incunabula is derived from a word signifying swaddling clothes, and the meaning has been transferred to the period of infancy in printing. It is a most interesting period when the

10 pt. (2 pt. leaded)

The period between the invention of printing in 1440 and 1500 is known as the Incunabula Period and books printed during that time are called Incunabula. The word Incunabula is derived from a word signifying swaddling clothes, and the meaning has been transferred to the period of infancy in

10 pt. (3 pt. leaded)

The period between the invention of printing in 1440 and 1500 is known as the Incunabula Period and books printed during that time are called Incunabula. The word Incunabula is derived from a word signifying swaddling clothes, and the meaning has been transferred to the period of infancy in

8 pt. solid

The period between the invention of printing in 1440 and 1500 is known as the Incunabula Period and books printed during that time are called Incunabula. The word Incunabula is derived from a word signifying swaddling clothes, and the meaning has been transferred to the period of infancy in printing. It is a most interesting period when the revival of learning found a great ally in the new invention of

8 pt. (1 pt. leaded)

The period between the invention of printing in 1440 and 1500 is known as the Incunabula Period and books printed during that time are called Incunabula. The word Incunabula is derived from a word signifying swaddling clothes, and the meaning has been transferred to the period of infancy in printing. It is a most interesting period when the revival of learning found a great ally in the new invention of

6 pt. solid

The period between the invention o printing in 1440 and 1500 is known as the Incunabula Period and books printed during that time are called Incunabula. The word Incunabula is derived from a word signifying swaddling clothes, and the meaning has been transferred to the period of infancy in printing. It is a most interesting period when the revival of learning found a great ally in the new invention of printing. Many of the

6 pt. (1 pt. leaded)

The period between the invention of printing in 1440 an 1500 is known as the Incunabula Period and books printed during that time are called Incunabula. The word Incunabula is derived from a word signifying swaddling clothes, and the meaning has been transferred to the period of infancy in printing. It is a most interesting period when the revival of

Clarendon

THE Clarendon types are now being used, perhaps more than ever before. They were originally designed to give bold emphasis, particularly for dictionaries so that the word defined stood out clearly. Clarendon type is still useful for that and similar purposes, but it is now being used in its own right. Moreover, with the increase in taste for the kind of letter a large range of sizes weights and widths has been cut.

In the normal weights there is only a slight difference between thick and thin strokes, but where curves join a stem the thin stroke is made thinner still. The serifs are almost as thick as the thick strokes, square ended and slightly bracketed so that one might call it a slab-serif type or Egyptian. Characteristic's of Clarendon are the even colour and a firm architectural precision.

Consort, from Stephenson Blake is a frank Victorian revival that deserves the success it has had this last few years.

Fortune, from the Bauer Typefoundry, Frankfurt, it is claimed is not a re-issue nor an adaption of the 1859 Bauer Clarendon. It is based on an original design by Dr. K. F. Bauer and Walter Baum. The light, bold, extra bold and bold italic comprise a useful range of weights so necessary in some forms of advertising. The extra bold is very rich in colour and robust in shape particularly effective for one or two words of display.

NEW CLARENDON: Series No. 617

ABCDEFG 72 pt.
HIJKLMN
OPQRSTU
VWXYZab
cdefghijkl
mnopqrtu
123456789

CONSORT: (Stephenson Blake)

36pt.

ABCDEFGHIJKLMN OPQRSTUVWXYZ&!
abcdefghijklmnopqrstu vwxyz *ABCDEFGHIJ KLMNOPQRSTUVWX YZ£ 123abcdefghijklm*

30pt. ABCDEFGHIJ abcdefghijkl

24pt. ABCDEFGHIJKLM abcdefehijkl

18pt. ABCDEFGHIJKLMNO abcdefghijklmnop

12pt. ABCDEFGHIJKLMNOPQRSTU abcdefghijklmnopqrstuv

10pt. ABCDEFGHIJKLMNOPQRSTUVWXYZ abcdefghijklmnopqrstuvwxyzæ

8pt. ABCDEFGHIJKLMNOPQRSTUVWXYZÆŒ 1234567890£$ abcdefghijklmnopqrstuvwxyz

6pt. ABCDEFGHIJKLMNOPQRSTUVWXYZÆŒ 1234567890 £$ abcdefghilmnopqrstuvwxyzæœfiffflffiffi&

CONSORT BOLD

36pt. **ABCD abc**

CONSORT CONDENSED

ABCDEF abcde

CONSORT BOLD CONDENSED

30pt. **ABCDEFG abcde**

CONSORT LIGHT

ABCDEabcd

FORTUNE EXTRA BOLD

ABCDEFG
HIJKLMN
abcdefghij
klmnopqrt

FORTUNE LIGHT

ABCDEFGHIJKL
MNOPQRSTUW
abcdefghijklmnop
qrstuvwxyz 12345

FORTUNE BOLD ITALIC

ABCDEFGHIJKLMNOPQ
abcdefghijklmnopqrstuvw

Garamond

THIS elegant type face is named after Claude Garamond, a distinguished seventeenth-century French typefounder. For a long time it was thought that Garamond was himself the designer but it is now established that the original from which this type was cut in 1922 was designed by Jean Jannon and shown in his specimen book of 1621.

It is one of the most venerable old faces, and though the design owes something to the early Venetian printers, more to Aldus then Jenson, the bluntish, bracketed serifs help to establish the characteristics we now know as Old Face. Many type designers have been influenced by it, and it is held in high repute by typographers and connoisseurs of letter forms.

The general tone is light, and appropriate to books where daintiness is required. Good press-work is important to retain the beauty of this face, owing to the very small counters in lower-case e and a, and cap A, which readily fill in when over-inked; and the type as a whole is apt to look pale and anæmic if under-inked. The tone varies in the different sizes as it does in many types. There is a noticeable increase in richness between the ordinary English 12 pt. and the 12 pt. Didot which is cast on English 13 pt. Then there is another big tonal increase in the 14 pt. The next jump is between 18 and 24 pt. which is very great, though in some types the difference is less pronounced.

It is an easy type to memorize owing to one or two strongly marked characteristics, e.g., cupped serifs in the lower-case; high cross-bar in cap A, making a smaller upper counter; E wider than the classic half a square; P, the lower arm of the bowl does not join the stem; T, left-hand arm serif at an angle, the right is vertical; W, the two inner strokes cross over; lower-case a and e are narrow, with small counters.

It is fairly narrow set, that is, many more words can fit into a given space in Garamond than in a wide-set type like Plantin or Scotch Roman. Also it has long ascenders and descender which make leading less necessary than in many types, and is pleasantly readable when set solid.

GARAMOND: Series No. 156

ABCDEFGM 72 pt.

HIJKLNOPS

QRTUVWX

YZ&:£abcdef

ghijklmnopqr

stuvwxyzfiffffffl

1234567890!?

GARAMOND: Series No. 156

72 pt. ANQRSW &

abcdefghijklmno

pqrstuvwxyz?ffl

60 pt. CAPS lower c *Ital*

48 pt. NOTE change *of the*

42 pt. WEIGHT between *sizes*

36 pt. THERE is a big jump *between*

30 pt. EIGHTEEN point & 24 pt. *Garamond*

24 pt. THERE ARE many swash letters as *AB*

18 pt. IN THIS FAMILY. Here are a few more sorts Qu st *Ri*

14 pt. THERE ARE ALSO some sizes like this which are cast *on the Didot point*

12D SYSTEM WHICH IS USED ON THE Continent but may also *be obtained on English*

13E
12D BODIES BUT VERY FEW PRINTERS stock these unusual sizes. *More FGKPYV*

GARAMOND: Series No. 156

HERE YOU SEE ELEVEN POINT CAP
lower case abcdefghijklmnopqrstuvwxyzabc

SMALL CAPS ABCDEFGHIJKLMNOPQRSTUVWXY 11 pt.
ITALIC CAPS Italic lower case abcdefghijklm

HERE YOU SEE TEN POINT CAPS ABCD
lower case abcdefghijklmnopqrstuvwxyzabcdef

SMALL CAPS ABCDEFGHIJKLMNOPQRSTUVWXYpAB 10 pt.
ITALIC CAPS Italic lower case abcdefghijklmnop

HERE YOU SEE EIGHT POINT CAPS ABCDEFJ
lower case abcdefghijklmnopqrstuvwxyzabcdefghijklm

SMALL CAPS ABCDEFGHIJKLMNOPQRSTUVWXYpABCDEFGHI 8 pt.
ITALIC CAPS Italic lower case abcdefghijklmnopqrstuvwx

12 pt. solid

at the top on *both* sides of the vertical strokes. Of this type Stanley Morison writes, 'No praise seems too high for it.' William Morris has copied it, so has Emery Walker, Cobden Sanderson and Bruce Rogers. Rather late in the century,

Compare the tone values of this column set solid

12 pt. (1 pt. leaded)

Aldus in 1495 brought out a tract by Cardinal Bembo in a type which is the ancestor of the large and important group of types known as old-face. It is much lighter in weight than Jenson's, the thin strokes are thinner in proportion

and this column which is 1 pt. leaded.

10 pt. solid

to the thick strokes, the serifs are bracketed, the cross-stroke of lower-case e is horizontal. Altogether this is one of the most admirable types that have ever been cast. From the Aldine types it is easy to see the derivation of present-day types through the intermediate stages of Garamond and Caslon. Even in so brief an outline of the history of type design one

Garamond is tolerable when solid

10 pt. (1 pt. leaded)

cannot omit to record that it was Aldus who introduced the kind of letter we know as italic. It was introduced for use, not as we do now for emphasis, but rather as a saver of space. Aldus brought out a series of pocket editions of the classics and devised italic type in order to get a greater number of words on to the page.

but becomes even lighter when leaded.

10 pt. (1½ pt leaded)

Altogether this is one of the most admirable types that have ever been cast. From the Aldine types it is easy to see the derivation of present-day types through the intermediate stages of Garamond and Caslon. Even in so brief an outline of the history of type design one

Compare both these columns

10 pt. (2 pt. leaded)

cannot omit to record that it was Aldus who introduced the kind of letter we know as italic. It was introduced for use, not as we do now for emphasis, but rather as a saver of space. Aldus brought out a series of pocket editions of the classics and devised italic type in order to

with Plantin & Times Roman.

8 pt. solid

It is regrettable that Aldus did not show the same good taste in italic that he had demonstrated with his roman letter, for his italic type (1501) has little to commend it when compared with Arrighi's lovely letter (1527). Aldine types influenced the great French printers like Simon de Colines and Robert Estienne, and the famous Garamond (1545). These French types in their turn

This is surprisingly legible when solid

8 pt. (1 pt. leaded)

influenced Dutch letter designers—noticeably Christopher Van Dyck (1660). At this time Dutch types gained an international reputation, so that it became a way of commending a book to say that it was printed in Dutch letter. Not only was the influence of the design felt in England, but type itself was imported. In 1683, Moxon,

but is better when leaded thus.

Gill Sans

GILL SANS, as it is usually called, is perhaps the finest of the sanserif group and sets a high standard of utilitarian dignity. It performs its useful tasks with an ease and grace which might be called urbane.

As the name suggests, this type was designed by Eric Gill. The forms of some of the capital letters first appeared on a fascia board over the bookshop in Bristol of Gill's friend, Douglas Cleverdon. This fascia was admired by Stanley Morison, typographer adviser to the Monotype Corporation, who commissioned Gill to complete the alphabet which was produced first in caps only (titling) in 1927. With foresight and faith, in spite of the clamour of disapproving printers on its first public appearance in 1928, lower-case and italics were cut, followed by a wide range of weights and varieties.

This type has a clean functional appearance that accords well with the austere tastes of the times and lends itself with commendable ease to the thousand-and-one jobs where continuous reading is not required. Completely at home in the advertising world, it has been employed experi-mentally in books where it has proved itself to be quite unsuitable for a novel or any form of long continuous text. A case might be made out for its use in modern poetry where long continuous reading is seldom called for, but to most literary people any Sans face seems cold and mechanistic, and there is no likelihood of even Gill Sans removing old-face types from their position of first favourites for books.

Gill Sans is a rather wide-set type which keeps it legible when the narrow-set sans becomes quite unreadable. The cap A has a sheared apex and the B has the lower bowl larger than the upper. E, F, S are the classic proportion of about half as wide as they are high. There is a typical curve to the tail of the R as it swings down from under the bowl, which is to be seen in nearly all Gill's alphabets. The lower-case a is normal in shape and has a certain amount of stress, that is, the line of the bowl thins as it enters the stem like a normal old-face letter. Suitable for most kinds of paper, it photographs well for line-blocks, photo-lithography, or photogravure.

GILL SANS TITLING: Series No. 231

ABCDEF

72 pt.

GHIJKLM

NOPQRS

TUVXYZ

W&1234

567890

GILL MEDIUM: Series No. 262

72 pt.

abcdefghijklt
mnopqrsuvx
wyzæœfififfiffl

ABGQRSMW!

abcdefghijkln
opqrstuvwxyz

60 pt.

CAP lower *Ital*

48 pt.

CAPS lower c *Italic*

GILL MEDIUM: Series No. 262

CAPS & lower case *Ital* 42 pt.

CAPITALS lower case *Italic* 36 pt.

CAPITALS & lower case *Italic* 123 30 pt.

CAPITALS and lower case *ITALIC* 123456 24 pt.

CAPITALS ABCDEFGHIJ abcdefghij *ABCDEFG abcdefg* 18 pt.

ABCDEFGHIJKLMNOPQ abcdefghijklmnopq *ABCDEFGHIJK abcdefghijk* 14 pt.

ABCDEFGHIJKLMNO abcdefghijklmnop *ABCDEFGHIJKLMNO abcdefghijklmnop* 12 pt.

12 pt. solid

the author of *Mechanic Exercises*, which treats of the craft of printing, refers to Dutch types in the following glowing terms: 'And for the commodious fatness they have beyond other letters, which easing the eyes in reading, renders them more legible; As also the true placing their Fats and Leans, with the sweet driving them into one another, and indeed all the accomplishment that can render

10 pt. solid

Letter regular and beautiful, do more visably appear in them than in any Letters by any other People; And therefore I think we may account the rules they were made by, to be rules of true shaped letter.' It was evidently these Dutch types which the famous Caslon used as

10 pt. (1½ pt. leaded)

a model. William Caslon I cut his ubiquitous Old Face between 1720 and 1726, and though there have been periods of neglect, it has been used and admired ever since. It was the first important type design to be produced in

8 pt. solid

England, and remains one of the finest. About the middle of the century, John Baskerville of Birmingham brought out a new type which differed in some respects from Caslon. The hairlines were thinner but not excessively thin, the distribution of weight in curved letters was rather more vertical than the typical old-face. Nevertheless, the serifs are inclined and bracketed,

8 pt. (1½ pt. leaded)

giving a general resemblance to old-face rather than modern. It is an open, comfortable type to read, with a distinct but not obtrusive individuality. At one time it was thought that Baskerville's letter had a direct influence on Bodoni, whose types brought to their logical conclusion those 'modern' tendencies which had

6 pt. solid

been creeping in for some time. Nowadays scholars are agreed that Bodoni would probably have designed as he did if Baskerville had never been born. But Baskerville was an innovator in other things which were certainly copied on the continent. His wove paper and method of hot-pressing his papers to give a smooth surface were imitated and enabled the thin serifs of Bodoni to be printed adequately. Bodoni, who was a printer in Parma in the late eighteenth century, produced a full-blooded modern type with the characteristic thin hairlines, fine unbracketed serifs and vertical stress in

6 pt. (1½ pt. leaded)

curved letters. These in their turn led to the 'fat-faces' which were so popular in posters in the early nineteenth century and which have had a revival in recent years. Modern-face types remained popular, even for the main text of books, during most of the Victorian era. But the contribution of Victorian designers to the history of type was not in text types but in decorative and often fantastic display types. Many of these, too, are enjoying a revival.

GILL BOLD: Series No. 275

72 pt. ABEGHSW

abcegirstw

AMRabcfrsp

GILL LIGHT: Series No. 362

72 pt. BEGHRSTW

abcefgmrstw

36 pt. *ABCDKMWabcdefghimprsw*

GILL MEDIUM CONDENSED: Series No. 485

24 pt. A B C D E F G H I J K L M N O P Q R S T U V W X Y Z £

a b c d e f g h i j k l m n o p q r s t u v w x y z ! ? ; -

GILL EXTRA BOLD: Series No. 321

ABFGRST

72 pt.

abcegrstw

GILL BOLD COND. TITLING NO. 1: Series No. 373

ABEGIRSN

72 pt.

GILL BOLD CONDENSED Series No. 343

ABDEGHRNW

72 pt.

abcdegnrstw

GILL SANSERIF SHADOW: Series No. 304

ABCEGKWXPRM

36 pt.

GILL SANSERIF SHADOW (1): Series No. 406

ABCDEGIKMPRWX

36 pt.

Granjon

GRANJON is available only for the Linotype machine. It is named after a celebrated publisher, printer, type-cutter and typefounder of the late sixteenth century who was still working in the early years of the seventeenth century. Although this type is named after Granjon the design is not his, but is based on the forms of Claude Garamont (or Garamond); in fact one authority describes Granjon as a true Garamond design. It was cut for the Linotype Company under the supervision of George W. Jones, a distinguished printer.

Without doubt one of the most satisfactory book types for 'slug' setting; slug being the name given to the solid line of type produced by the Linotype, Intertype, or Ludlow machine. It is clear and legible, combines well into a page, and has charm and poise.

It is not easy for the beginner to differentiate from Garamond, but a careful comparison will make the differences evident. The cap A is not quite so narrow, nor the cross-bar quite so high as in the 'MONOTYPE' Garamond. The serifs of lower-case i, j, m, n are not so cupped in Granjon.

GRANJON: Linotype

ABCDEFGHIJKLMN 48 pt.

OPQRSTUVWXYZ &

CAPS ONLY IN 42 PT: 42 pt.

CAPS AND lower case in 36pt 36 pt.

abcdefghijklmnopqrstuvwxyz &

CAPS AND lower case but no italic 30 pt.

CAPITALS and lower case *and Italic also in* 24 pt.

ITALIC abcdefghijklmnopqrstuvwxyz&12345

CAPITALS 1234567890 lower case and *Italic lower case* 18 pt.

HERE YOU SEE LINOTYPE GRANJON in action. This line is about *right for size* 14 pt.

BUT HERE THE MEASURE is too great for the size. *A shorter line would be much better* 12 pt.

HERE YOU SEE TEN POINT CAPS ABCD
lower case abcdefghijklmnopqrstuvwxyz 123456

SMALL CAPS ABCDEFGHIJKLMNOPQRSTUVWXYZ ABCDEF 10 pt.
ITALIC CAPS italic lower case abcdefghijklmn

HERE YOU SEE EIGHT POINT CAPS ABCDEFGHIJK
lower case abcdefghijklmnopqrstuvwxyzæœfiflffffiffl12345

SMALL CAPS ABCDEFGHIJKLMNOPQRSTUVWXYZÆŒ ,.:; *†‡§‖¶!? 8 pt.
ITALIC CAPS lower case abcdefghijklmnopqrstuvwxyz&

HERE YOU SEE SIX POINT CAPS ABCDEFGHIJKLMNOPQRSTUVW
and lower case abcdefghijklmnopqrstuvwxyzæœ fiflffffiffl !? 1234567890

THESE ARE THE SMALL CAPS ABCDEFGHIJKLMNOPQRSTUVWXYZÆŒ ,.:; *†‡§‖¶ 6 pt.
ITALIC CAPS and lower case abcdefghijklmnopqrstuvwxyzæœfiflffffiffl

10 pt. solid

We too easily lose sight of the fact that printing was not merely one of the key inventions of the modern technical era, far more significant in every way than was the invention of the steam engine, but that at a very early period it set the pattern for the application of the machine to all the other arts. Printing was the first of modern arts to introduce

10 pt. (2 pt. leaded)

We too easily lose sight of the fact that printing was not merely one of the key inventions of the modern technical era, far more significant in every way than was the invention of the steam engine, but that at a very early period it set the pattern for the application of the machine to all the other arts.

Grotesque

THE Grotesque types have been enjoying a vogue for many years now and seems likely to continue for a long time to come. They have a clear, crisp, rational appearance that makes them so appropriate for layouts in the Bauhams tradition. Although interest in Grotesque and the other sans-serif types has been growing since the 1920's, it was Edward Johnston with his sans for the London Underground (now London Transport) which probably sparked off the flame.

But Grotesque letters, both expanded and condensed are revivals of nineteenth century custom. Throughout the nineteenth century examples can be found of printers using these types and the same form of letter appeared on chapels, hospitals, public baths, breweries and taverns which still exist and are often very well designed and suited to the building they embellish.

It is difficult to say just what precise constitutes a 'Grotesque', but Grotesque No 8 is typical. The set is wide and letters like B, E, F are much wider than the classical proportions. There is usually a spur at the bottom of the straight stroke of capital G and the tail of R tends towards a double curve.

As the specimens make it plain to see the weights vary from very light to very heavy. Although most Grots are wide a number are condensed, indeed, some are extremely condensed.

The x height is usually very great, that is, both ascenders and decenders are short. This makes most Grots appear very big on the body.

GROTESQUE No. 8 (Stephenson Blake)

ABCDEFI
72 pt.

GHIKLMNO
60 pt.

OPQRSTUVW
48 pt.

WXYZ123456789
36 pt.

abcdefgh
72 pt.

jklmnopqrs
60 pt.

tuvwxyz&£P!
48 pt.

AISO in 30pt 24 POINT type

THIS IS SIX POINT abcdefghijklmnopq THIS IS 12 POINT abcdefg

GROTESQUE No. 9 (Stephenson Blake)

72 pt.

ABCDEFGHIJ

60 pt.

GHIKLMNO

48 pt.

STUVWXYZ123

4567890£&!([

72 pt.

abcdefghij

60 pt.

jklmnopqrst

48 pt.

vwxyz-.,:;aeae....

ALSO in 30 point 24 POINT ABabcd

THIS IS SIX POINT abcdefghijklmnopqrst   THIS IS 12 POINT abcdefghijkl

GROTESQUE No. 10 (Stephenson Blake)

ABCDEFGHIKLM 42 pt.

MNOPQRSTUVWXYZ 30 pt.

abcdefghijklmnopq 42 pt.

pqstuvwxyz12345678?! 30 pt.

ABCDEFGHIJabcdefghijklmnop 24 pt.

MONOTYPE GROTESQUE No. 1 BOLD

ABCDEFGHIJKLMNOPQRSTUVWXYZ
abcdefghijklmnopqrstuvwxyz

NARROW GROTESQUE (Haas)

ABCDEFGHIJKLMNOPQRSTUVWXYZ
abcdefghijklmnopqrstuvwxyz 1234567890 ·

GROTESQUE No. 4 (Stephenson Blake)

LMNOPQRSTUV
YZ1234567890,;:?!&
THERE IS NO LOWER CASE

Imprint

IMPRINT is a modest, self-effacing, old-face letter cut in December, 1912, and first used in *The Imprint*, a typographic journal whose influence is not yet exhausted through the standard it set of scholarship in printing history, of aesthetic discrimination and of the maintenance of technical excellence.

Four men have a claim to be its designers or sponsors or instigators—it is hard to know what to call them to be strictly correct. They are J. H. Mason, Edward Johnston, Ernest Jackson and Gerard Meynell. The design is frankly based on Caslon, and it is a fair description to call it Caslon adapted to the mechanical composing machine and to machine printing on smooth, dry paper. This last point must not be overlooked, because the original Caslon was designed for printing on damp, hand-made, comparatively rough paper which thickens the letter. On smooth, dry paper Caslon looks thin, and in Imprint this weakness is corrected by a slight increase in weight. Imprint is said to be the first good type to be designed (or should one say adapted?) to modern mechanical conditions.

In general, Imprint has the qualities that used to be ascribed to the perfect servant. It has no pronounced idiosyncrasies (which are sometimes described as individuality) and it does its job without attracting attention to itself. In other words, it has many attributes of the ideal type, and will continue to give satisfactory service like the good and faithful servant it is.

Apart from a general resemblance to Caslon the cap K is perhaps the best letter to identify this type. There is a comparatively long horizontal stroke connecting the junction of the arm and tail. The lower-case k has a curved arm, and the tail joins the arm some distance from the stem. The upper arm of the bowl of the cap C has a barb while the lower arm finishes with a point.

The italic is fairly wide set and is stronger in colour than most old-face italics, which makes Imprint italic remarkably legible and readable.

IMPRINT: Series No. 101

ABCDEFGHIKLM 48 pt.
NOPQRSTUVWX
YZ&!?£abcdefghijkl
mnopqrstuvwxyzfifl
uvy 1234567890 *wxz*
ABCDEFGHIJK
abcdefghijklmnopqr
ABCDEFGHIJKLMNQ 36 pt.
abcdefghjklmnopqrstuvw
abcdefghijklmnopqrstuvwx
ROMAN & *ITALIC CAPS* 30 pt.
roman lower case and *italic lower*

IMPRINT: Series No. 101

24 pt. ROMAN CAPS & *ITALIC CAPS*
roman lower case and *italic lower case*

18 pt. ROMAN CAPS AND ALSO *ITALIC CAPITAL*
roman lower case and also *italic lower case is available*

14 pt. ABCDEFGHIJKLMNOPQRST   *ABCDEFGHIJKLMNOPQRST*
abcdefghijklmnopqrstuvwxyzfifflfffffi   *abcdefghijklmnopqrstuvwxyzfifflffffffi*

12 pt. ABCDEFGHIJKLMNOPQRSTUVW SMALL CAPS ABCDEFGHIJKLMNOPQRSTUV
ower case abcdefghijklmnopqrstuvwxyz *ITALIC ABCDEFGHIJKabcdefghijk*

12 pt. solid

A question students frequently ask of an instructor, or of themselves, is "How
may I know a good type when I see one?" It is a reasonable question to ask,
and almost as difficult to answer as "How may I know a good man when I see
him?" The question on type is easier, at least in this, that one may get wider
agreement as to what a type is for, than the profounder and more controversial
subject "What is mankind for?" Once you are agreed as to what a thing is for,
the goodness or success of the thing will depend on whether or not it fulfils the

12 pt. (1 pt. leaded)

A question students frequently ask of an instructor, or of themselves, is "How
may I know a good type when I see one?" It is a reasonable question to ask,
and almost as difficult to answer as "How may I know a good man when I see
him?" The question on type is easier, at least in this, that one may get wider
agreement as to what a type is for, than the profounder and more controversial
subject "What is mankind for?" Once you are agreed as to what a thing is for,
the goodness or success of the thing will depend on whether or not it fulfils the

12 pt. (2 pt. leaded)

A question students frequently ask of an instructor, or of themselves, is "How
may I know a good type when I see one?" It is a reasonable question to ask,
and almost as difficult to answer as "How may I know a good man when I see
him?" The question on type is easier, at least in this, that one may get wider
agreement as to what a type is for, than the profounder and more controversial
subject "What is mankind for?" Once you are agreed as to what a thing is for,
the goodness or success of the thing will depend on whether or not it fulfils the

IMPRINT: Series No. 101

HERE YOU SEE ELEVEN POINT CAPS
lower case abcdefghijklmnopqrstuvwxyzab
HERE YOU SEE TEN POINT CAPS ABCD
lower case abcdefghijklmnopqrstuvwxyzabcde
HERE YOU SEE EIGHT POINT CAPS ABCDEF
lower case abcdefghijklmnopqrstuvwxyzabcdefghijkl
HERE YOU SEE SIX POINT CAPS ABCDEFGHIJKLM
lower case abcdefghijklmnopqrstuvwxyzabcdefghijklmnopqrstu

SMALL CAPS ABCDEFGHIJKLMNOPQRSTUVWXYZ
ITALIC CAPS Italic lower case abcdefghijk 11 pt.
SMALL CAPS ABCDEFGHIJKLMNOPQRSTUVWXYZABC
ITALIC CAPS Italic lower case abcdefghijklmn 10 pt.
SMALL CAPS ABCDEFGHIJKLMNOPQRSTUVWXYZABCDEFGH
ITALIC CAPS Italic lower case abcdefghijklmnopqrst 8 pt.
SMALL CAPS ABCDEFGHIJKLMNOPQRSTUVWXYZABCDEFGHIJKLMNOPQ
ITALIC CAPS Italic lower case abcdefghijklmnopqrstuvwxyzabc 6 pt.

12 pt. solid

A question students frequently ask of an instructor, or of themselves, is "How may I know a good type when I see one?" It is a reasonable question to ask and almost as difficult to answer as "How may I know

12 pt. (1 pt. leaded)

A question students frequently ask of an instructor, or of themselves, is "How may I know a good type when I see one?" It is a reasonable question to ask and almost as difficult to answer as "How may I know

12 pt. (2 pt. leaded)

A question students frequently ask of an instructor, or of themselves, is "How may I know a good type when I see one?" It is a reasonable question to ask and almost as diffi-

12 pt. (3 pt. leaded)

A question students frequently ask of an instructor, or of themselves, is "How may I know a good type when I see one?" It is a reasonable question to ask and almost as diffi-

10 pt. solid

A question students frequently ask of an instructor, or of themselves, is "How may I know a good type when I see one?" It is a reasonable question to ask and almost as difficult to answer as "How may I know a good man when I see him?" The question on typeis easier, at least in this, that one may get wider agreement as to what a type is for, than the profounder and more controversial

10 pt. (1 pt. leaded)

A question students frequently ask of an instructor, or of themselves, is "How may I know a good type when I see one?" It is a reasonable question to ask and almost as difficult to answer as "How may I know a good man when I see him?" The question on type is easier, at least in this, that one may get wider agreement as to what a type is for,

8 pt. solid

A question students frequently ask of an instructor, or of themselves, is "How may I know a good type when I see one?" It is a reasonable question to ask and almost as difficult to answer as "How may I know a good man when I see him?" The question on type is easier, at least in this, that one may get wider agreement as to what a type is for, than the profounder and more controversial subject "What is mankind for?" Once you are agreed as to what a thing is for, the goodness or success of the thing

8 pt. (1 pt. leaded)

A question students frequently ask of an instructor, or of themselves, is "How may I know a good type when I see one?" It is a reasonable question to ask and almost as difficult to answer as "How may I know a good man when I see him?" The question on type is easier, at least in this, that one may get wider agreement as to what a type is for, than the profounder and more controversial subject "What is mankind for?" Once you are agreed as to what

Perpetua

PERPETUA is a type cut in 1929 by the Monotype Corporation from designs by Eric Gill, and was the name of a female saint martyred at Carthage in A.D. 203 with a companion Felicity, who is remembered in the name of an italic letter by Gill.

It is one of the most distinguished types now available and is original in a way that many recent good types are not, some being frankly revivals, others admittedly derivative. The capitals have an inscriptional quality that recalls Gill's long experience as a letter-cutter in stone.

It is not large on the body and in consequence can be used effectively without leading in the text sizes, that is from 14 pt. down. While not so versatile as Baskerville and Bembo, it can yet be used for a wide variety of jobs and is particularly suitable for books where dignity, repose and stateliness are required. It is admirable for book jackets where the related Bold and Bold Titling are specially useful. It is also useful in press advertising.

The serifs are finely pointed and require a smooth paper to bring out the clean brilliance of the design, but it is not suitable for art paper except in the large sizes and, of course, the bold weight. The A has a horizontal sheared apex. B, D, E have classic proportions and the counters have no bracket to the junction of arm to stem at the top, but have a generous curve where the bottom arm springs from the stem. There is a typical 'Gill' curve to the tail of cap R where the tail swings from the stem under the bowl. T has upward projecting spurs at the end of the arms. Lower-case a has a pointed terminal to the arch very reminiscent of stonemasons' letters. A flatness at the foot of the bowl of d where it joins the stem and continues into the serif is unusual.

In the italic B, D, P, R have a kind of rising serif at the top which continues uninterrupted into the curve of the bowl. The g has a long straight stem with a full o-height bowl, this time reminiscent of calligraphy rather than stone-cutting. Oblique feet distinguish p and q.

PERPETUA TITLING: Series No. 258

A B C D E F

72 pt.

G H I J K L M

N O P Q R S

T U V W X Y

Z & £ ?! 1 2 3

4 5 6 7 8 9 0

PERPETUA: Series No. 239

72 pt. abcdefghjklmn
iopqrstuvwxyz
&£ABCEHRSO

abcdefghijklmn
opqrstuvwxyzffi-

60 pt. CAPS lower c *Ital*

48 pt. NOTE change in *weight*

42 pt. FROM one size to *another*

36 pt. THERE is a big change *in weight*

PERPETUA: Series No. 239

BETWEEN this 30 point *Perpetua and* 30 pt.

THIS 24 POINT, which is *very much lighter* 24 pt.

SUCH DIFFERENCES of weight vary between *different types* 18 pt.

THUS IN THE SMALLER SIZES OF
be obtained which give a variety of
IT IS SOMETIMES MUCH BETTER TO
than the caps of a smaller size of type.
EFFECTIVE AND HAS HISTORICAL ABCDGHIKE
lower case only, and so roman or upright caps abcde
CAPITALS AND SMALL CAPITALS ARE USUALLY
rare occasions should lower case or italic be letter-spaced
SMALL SIZES NEED SHORTER LINES (MEASURES)ABCDEFG
nd other similar occasions. The proportions of the small abcdfeg

MOST TYPES SMALL CAPS LIKE THIS CAN
tone and texture on the one body size. 14 pt.
USE SMALL CAPS OF A LARGER SIZE RATHER
Italic lower case and small caps are sometimes 12 pt.
PRECEDENT BECAUSE ITALIC WAS FIRST CUT IN ABCDEF
were used when capital letters were necessary abcdefghijklmn 10 pt.
IMPROVED BY LETTER-SPACING, BUT ONLY ON VERY ABCDEFG
spaced. Leading improves the small sizes of most types. abcdefghijk 8 pt.
THESE SIX POINT SMALL CAPITALS HAVE THEIR USE IN FOOTNOT
sizes are not identical with those of the large sizes. abcdefghijklmnopqrst 6 pt.

12 pt. solid

A question students frequently ask of an
instructor, or of themselves, is " How
may I know a good type when I see one ? "
This is a reasonable question to ask and
is almost as difficult to answer as " How
may I know a good man when I see him ? "

Compare the tone value of this column set solid

10 pt. solid

A question students, frequently as of an instructor,
or of themselves, is " How may I know a good type
when I see one ? " This is a reasonable question to ask
and almost as difficult to answer as " How may I
know a good man when I see him ? " The question
on type is easier, at least in this, that one may get
wider agreement as to what a type is for, than the
profounder and more controversial subject " What

Perpetua is tolerable when solid

8 pt. solid

A question students frequently ask of an instructor, or of
themselves' is " How may I know a good type when I see
one ? " This is a reasonable question to ask and almost as
difficult to answer as " How may I know a good man when
I see him ? " The question on type is easier, at least in
this, that one may get wider agreement as to what a type
is for, than the profounder and more controversial subject
" What is mankind for ? " Once you are agreed as to
what a thing is for, the goodness or success of the thing will

This size appears leaded when solid

12 pt. (1 pt. leaded)

A question students frequently ask of an
instructor, or of themselves, is " How
may I know a good type when I see one ? "
This is a reasonable question to ask and
is almost as difficult to answer as " How
may I know a good man when I see him ? "

and this column which is one point leaded

10 pt. (1 pt. leaded)

A question students frequently ask of an instructor,
or of themselves, is " How may I know a good type
when I see one ? " This is a reasonable question to ask
and almost as difficult to answer as " How may I
know a good man when I see him ? " The question
on type is easier, at least in this, that one may get
wider agreement as to what a type is for, than the

but appears lighter in tone when leaded

8 pt. (1 pt. leaded)

A question students frequently ask of an instructor, or of
themselves, is " How may I know a good type when I see
one ? " This is a reasonable question to ask and almost as
difficult to answer as " How may I know a good man when
I see him ? " The question on type is easier, at least in
this, that one may get wider agreement as to what a type
is for, than the profounder and more controversial subject
" What is mankind for ? " Once you are agreed as to

and is even lighter when leaded

PERPETUA TITLING: Series No. 258

60 pt. "A LOVE OF

48 pt. LETTERS IS THE

42 pt. BEGINNING OF

36 pt. TYPOGRAPHICAL

30 pt. WISDOM. THAT IS, THE

24 pt. LOVE OF LETTERS AS LITERA-

18 pt. TURE AND THE LOVE OF LETTERS AS

14 pt. PHYSICAL ENTITIES, HAVING ABSTRACT BEAUTY

12 pt. OF THEIR OWN, APART FROM THE IDEAS THEY MAY

10 pt. EXPRESS OR THE EMOTIONS THEY MAY EVOKE." JOHN. R. BIGGS. 1940

PERPETUA BOLD: Series No. 461

72 pt. AB ab   KLM lmno 42 p

60 pt. DEI dfe   NOPT pqrst 36 p

                        QRSUV uvwxy 30 p

48 pt. FGH ghik   WXYZ?& abcdefgh 24 p

                        1234567890£ ijklmnopqrs 18 p

PERPETUA LIGHT TITLING: Series No. 480

ABCDEFG 72 pt.

HJKLMNOP 60 pt.

QRSTUVWXY 48 pt.

Z&1234567890 42 pt.

THIS IS ELEGANT BUT 36 pt.

NOT AFFECTED. IS ADMIRABLE 24 pt.

FOR THE INITIAL LETTERS OF CHAPTERS 18 pt.

HERE it is in use with 12 pt. Times, 3 pt. leaded. Another occasion where Perpetua Light Titling can be used with distinction is on a title-page where the title may be one short word, for example, EMMA or EGO. A large size of the normal weight is too heavy for some tastes but the Light Titling gives size, and the decorative value that goes with a few letters in a large size, without being blatant.

The Bold Titling which can be obtained in 12 and 14 pt. as well as the sizes shown finds appropriate employment on Book jackets, in Press advertisements, leaflets and brochures where boldness is required to be associated with dignity.

Plantin

THIS type is one of the few types specially designed to look well when printed on art paper. It is named after Christopher Plantin, one of the most distinguished printer-publishers the world has known. The family of the Plantins continued to print in Antwerp for almost three centuries, some relative of the original Plantin carrying on the tradition with varying skill and distinction. The Plantin's printing office is now preserved intact as a museum (it has even survived the 1939-45 war) where prints from the old type were being made up to the outbreak of war in 1939.

Plantin, Monotype Series 110, not to be confused with typefounders' (Shanks) Plantin, is large on the body, strong in colour, and is therefore admirable for children's books. It also survives the thin ink of high-speed newspaper machines which makes it a good choice for setting the 'body matter' (other than display lines) of advertisements. Ideal for the text of art-paper folders, magazines, etc. Its characteristics are sheared apex to cap A, the stem of which projects slightly to the left. Splayed M. The bowl of the P does not quite join up with the stem. Sheared terminal of cap C, G, S. The two inside strokes of cap W cross over. Blunt terminal at head of lower-case a. Short descenders. Wedge serifs at head of b, d, h, k, l, and i, j, m, n, p, r.

The design itself is not based on any design of Plantin's but on a fount which recent researches prove to have been cut either by Garamond or Granjon. The Monotype first issued Plantin 110 in 1913.

PLANTIN: Series No. 110

H B abst *Dc* 72 pt.

CDE efghi *Aab* 60 pt.

FGHJ jklmn *hjklm* 48 pt.

KLMN opqrsu *nopqst* 42 pt.

OPQRS tvwxyz1 *uvwxyz* 36 pt.

TUVWXY 23456789 *&?! abcd* 30 pt.

Z&£?!ABCD 0:;-(ffifflffffifl *efghijklmno* 24 pt.

EFGHIJKLMNP abcdefghijklmno *pqrstuvwxyz &* 18 pt.

OQRSTUVWXYZAB pqrstuwxyz abcdefg *abcdefghijklmnopqrs* 14 pt.

CDEFGHIJKLMNOPQR hijklmnopqrstuvwxyz 12 *tuvwxyz &?! abcdefghij* 12 pt.

STUVWXYZ &£?! ABCDEFG 34567890ffifffifffiffabcdefghijkl *klmnopqrstuvwxyz&abcdef* 11 pt.

HIJKLMNOPQRSTUVWXYZ £ abcdefghijklmnopqrstuvwxyzab *ghijklmnopqrstuvwxyz&£!?* 10 pt.

ABCDEFGHIJKLMNOPQRSTU cdefghijklmnopqrstuvwxyz 1234 *abcdefghijklmnopqrstuvwxyz* 9 pt.

VWXYZ &£!? ABCDEFGHIJKLMN 567890abcdefghijklmnopqrstuvwxy *bcdefghijklmnopqrstuvwxyz&abc* 8 pt.

OQRSTUVWXYZABCDEFGHIJKLMN£! abcdefghijklmnopqrstuvwxyz!ffifflfifi12345 *defghijklmnopqrstuvwxyz &£!?abcdefgh* 6 pt.

11 pt. solid

A question students frequently ask of an instructor, or of themselves, is " How may I know a good type when I see one ? " It is a reasonable question to ask and almost as difficult to answer as " How may I know a good man when I see him ? " The

11 pt. (2½ pt. leaded)

A question students frequently ask of an instructor, or of themselves, is " How may I know a good type when I see one ? " It is a reasonable question to ask and almost as difficult to answer as " How may I know

Rockwell

Rockwell is one of the most readily obtained slab-serif letters, and though somewhat dull in design is a useful type for a wide variety of commercial work. The different weights, together with the 'condensed' and 'shadow' versions, are advantageous where there is a need to differentiate visually between prices, names, code numbers, headings, sub-headings, sub-sub-headings and the like, without losing a sense of unity.

Rockwell is almost monotone, but there is a slight thinning where the bowl of lower-case a joins the upright stem. Cap A has a conspicuous serif projecting on *both* sides of the apex. Cap C has a serif on the upper arm but not on the lower. G is practically a circle. Cap E and F are fairly wide. Lower-case g is almost a lower-case o with a tail on, and e also is nearly a circle broken by the horizontal stroke.

ROCKWELL MEDIUM: Series No. 371

ABCDEFJ 72 pt.

GHIJKLM

NOPQRS

TUVWXY

Z&£?123

4567890

ROCKWELL MEDIUM: Series No. 371

72 pt.

abcdefghij
klmnopqrs
tuvwxyzfifl

60 pt.

CAPS lower c

48 pt.

CAPS lower *Italic*

ABCDEGKMRW

abcdefghiklmn

opqrstuvwxyz

ROCKWELL MEDIUM: Series No. 371

CAPS lower & *Italic* 42 pt.

EGYPTIAN is one *name* 36 pt.

THAT HAS been used *for* 30 pt.

THIS FORM of letter. *Slab-serif is* 24 pt.

A MORE descriptive term. *Italic is a sloped* 18 pt.

ROMAN LETTER, BUT the l.c. roman g *might be called* 14 pt.

AN UPRIGHT ITALIC LETTER owing to the absence of the *closed loop* 12 pt.

THIS IS NOT A BEAUTIFUL type but it has its uses in some *kinds of advertising* 10 pt.

BOOKS HAVE BEEN SET IN Rockwell where there is very little text *but a lot of photographs.* Any 8 pt.

LENGTH OF TEXT SET IN A SLAB-serif type is extremely tiresome indeed Six point *Rockwell light bold roman italic medium* 6 pt.

12 pt. solid

A question students frequently ask of an instructor, or of themselves, is " How may I know a good type when I see one ? " It is a reasonable question to ask and almost as difficult to answer

12 pt. (1 pt. leaded)

A question students frequently ask of an instructor, or of themselves, is " How may I know a good type when I see one ? " It is a reasonable question to ask and almost as difficult to answer

10 pt. solid

A question students frequently ask of an instructor, or of themselves, is " How may I know a good type when I see one ? " It is a reasonable question to ask and almost as difficult to answer as " How may I know a good man when I see him ? " The question on type is easier, at least in this, that one may get

10 pt. (1 pt. leaded)

A question students frequently ask of an instructor, or of themselves, is " How may I know a good type when I see one ? " It is a reasonable question to ask and almost as difficult to answer as " How may I know a good man when I see him ? " The question on type is

8 pt. solid

A question students ask frequently of an instructor, or of themselves, is " How may I know a good type when I see one ? " It is a reasonable question to ask and almost as difficult to answer as " How may I know a good man when I see him ? " The question on type is easier, at least in this, that one may get wider agreement as to what a type is for, than the profounder and more controversial subject " What is mankind for ? " Once you are

8 pt. (1 pt. leaded)

A question students ask frequently of an instructor, or of themselves, is " How may I know a good type when I see one ? " It is a reasonable question to ask and almost as difficult to answer as " How may I know a good man when I see him ? " The question on type is easier, at least in this, that one may get wider agreement as to what a type is for, than the profounder and more controversial

ROCKWELL MEDIUM CONDENSED: Series No. 414

ABC abci
72 pt.

OPQRST stuvwxy 36 p

DEF defg
60 pt.

T U V W X Y Z & (!) 30 p

GHIJK hjklmn
48 pt.

1 2 3 4 5 6 7 8 9 0 £ 24 p

THOMAS BEWICK also an artist 18 p

NATURALIST AND engraver was thought 14 p

ROCKWELL LIGHT: Series No. 390

ABab
72 pt.

JKLNjklm 42 p

CD cdi
60 pt.

MOPnopqr 36 p

QRST stuvw £ 30 p

FGH fgh
48 pt.

UVWX xyz ff ffi ffl 24 p

YZ&ABCD? 1234567890 18 p

12 POINT type   10 POINT type here

6 POINT TYPE also here   8 POINT TYPE is here

ROCKWELL SHADOW: Series No. 175

72 pt.   60   48   42   36   30   24   18   72 p

ABCWRHSmE

ABat
CDcd
FGNefg

2 pt.
0 pt.
8 pt.

ROCKWELL BOLD: Series No. 391

HKLhlen 42 pt.

MNOmor 36 pt.

PQRST pqrtu 30 pt.

UVWXYvwxyza 24 pt.

Z 1234567890 £&ffifflfifl 18 pt.

12 POINT type   10 POINT type

6 POINT TYPE here also a   8 POINT type here

ROCKWELL BOLD CONDENSED: Series No. 359

ABCab
DEGcdei
HIJK fghjk

2 pt.
0 pt.
8 pt.

LMNOlmnot 42 pt.

PQRST pqrsuv 36 pt.

UVWXYZ wxyzabcdef 24 pt.

ABCDEFGHI ghijklmnopqrst 18 pt.

1234567890 £?!:;& ffi ffl fl ff fi 14 pt.

ROCKWELL EXTRA BOLD: Series No. 424

BCDE abcdefg .

FGHIKOP hlmnprst,?

8 pt.
4 pt.

NOPQRST qrstuvwxyz 12 pt.

UVXYZ & abcdefghijklno 10 pt.

1234567890 abcdefghijklmnop 8 pt.

Times

This is one of the most successful typographic creations of this century, for it is in no sense a revival as are so many of the best types issued during the last twenty-five years. So many people had a say in this important design that to state categorically that it was the work of one man would be untrue. Yet nobody would deny that the man who had the biggest say and whose authority and influence were the most far reaching was Stanley Morison.

When *The Times* decided to restyle their newspaper, experiments were made with many types and for a time Baskerville was highly favoured. A special 9 pt. Perpetua was cut and finally abandoned for an entirely new design made to suit the requirements of modern newspaper where thin inks are used at high speed. In April, 1931, proofs, printed on a rotary press were made from a 9 pt. size and carefully scrutinized by 'a distinguished ophthalmic authority' and others, whose recommendations were acted upon in subsequent trials.

It is one of the most useful 'bread-and-butter' types we possess, and is equally appropriate in books and advertising. Large on the body and strong in colour, it successfully survives the attenuating ordeal of being printed on art paper. Special long ascenders and descenders are made which render Times suitable for book production, but normally it requires leading; for example, the 10 pt. is best on a 12 pt. body, the 12 pt. on a 14 pt. body.

Being an old-face, the point of maximum stress is at an angle; in the lower-case e and c the stress is almost on the base line. Cap A has a pointed apex; the upper arm of C has a barbed beak, the lower arm ends in a point; the vertical part rising from the lower arm of G is long (too long, perhaps). The lower arm of the bowl of P turns slightly up as it rejoins the stem.

The upright or roman is economical of space, but the italic is fairly wide set as italics go, though it is thereby very legible. Notice that the Series 327, which includes the normal text sizes, ranges from $4\frac{1}{4}$ pt. to 48 pt., and thus there is no lower-case above 48 pt. The larger sizes are in titling. The varying weights and widths make Times almost a universal type.

Times Bold has horizontal serifs at the head of lower-case letters like h, l, k, m, n, so that it might be classed as a modern. Times Bold ranges from $5\frac{1}{2}$ pt. to 72 pt., so there are large sizes of lower-case in Bold.

TIMES ROMAN: Series No. 327

ABCDEFGHIJK 48 pt.
LMNOPQRSTU
VWXYZ&£?!..,;:()-
1234567890
abcdefghijklmnop
qrstuvwxyzfflffffffffi

CAPS lower but no italic 36 pt.

CAPS AND lower case only 30 pt.

CAPS & lower case and *ITALIC also* 24 pt.

A PURITAN may go to his brown-*Bread crust* 18 pt.

WITH AS GROSS an appetite as *ever an alderman*

TO HIS TURTLE. NOT that food which entereth *into the mouth* 14 pt.

DEFILETH A MAN, but the appetile with which *it is eaten.* *H. D. Thoreau* 12 pt.

NOTE: HERE long descenders are employed g j p q y also *IN italic g j p q y.*

TIMES ROMAN: Series No. 327

12 pt. solid

and there is a tendency for some artists to imitate Victorian title-pages with the titles and authors' names involved as part of the picture— the letters themselves often being stunted, contorted trees and the like.

11 pt. solid

aesthetic standards in the crafts. Prominent among the prophets crying in an artistic wilderness and striving to turn it into a paradise was William Morris. He founded his Kelmscott Press in order to produce the Book Beautiful. He found his inspiration

10 pt. solid

things and most of them he did well, and though no book designer today would use the heavy types, the closely-packed lines, the luxuriant borders of Kelmscott volumes, all respect the ideas for which Morris struggled and the vigour with which he fought. Shortly

9 pt. solid

page; Emery Walker's trim tomes were as solemn as a judge, and the most ornament he would allow himself was an occasional coloured initial. Self-discipline was exercised to the point of asceticism. But the Doves severity was a good counterblast to the Kelmscott exuberance, and

8 pt. solid

catered for a wealthy few. In the twentieth century one of the most influential men in letter design was Edward Johnston, a calligrapher of genius, whose work, though small in quantity, bears comparison with the great scribes of the Middle Ages. Johnston's most influential *type* is the sanserif he designed for

6 pt. solid

prepared for good craftsmanship and artistry when it appeared. It was after the 1914-18 war that there came a big improvement in printing in England and when good types began to be available for general use. (Kelmscott types were of course private, and in any case had little commercial value, and the Doves type came to a tragic end in the Thames at Hammersmith.) With Stanley Morison as typographic adviser, the Monotype Corporation began to put on the market well-cut revivals of old types

12 pt. (1 pt. leaded)

After much shoddy typography came a great revival in the '90s. There was a general reaction, by many cultured people, against the ugliness of industrial England and the absence of

11 pt. (1 pt. leaded)

in the fifteenth century and modelled his books on the general plan of the fifteenth-century Italian books. He imitated Jenson's type, though some people might regard it as a travesty. William Morris did many

10 pt. (1 pt. leaded)

after, Cobden Sanderson and Emery Walker set up the Doves Press with similar high ideals but produced books totally different in appearance. Morris's books teemed with decoration that almost literally spilled off the

9 pt. (1 pt. leaded)

the two presses and their work mark the beginning of a typographic renaissance of which we are feeling the benefit today. Men are now trying to produce books for the many with something of the zeal and idealism with which William Morris, Cobden Sanderson and Emery Walker

8 pt. (1 pt. leaded)

the Underground Railways—a letter so different from the medieval hands he loved to write. But it was Johnston the man and teacher, and his book *Writing and Illuminating and Lettering*, that had such a far-reaching effect. He made so many people care for and love good writing and lettering, that the ground was

6 pt. (1 pt. leaded)

selected with taste supported by considerable knowledge. Before the 1914-18 war there were only two or three good types available for printers—types like Caslon, Fry's Baskerville, which had to be hand-set, and Imprint, which had been cut for machine-setting just before the war. When the recent war started in 1939 that number had grown to at least twenty-five or more. A large number of these types are frankly revivals dug out of the past,

TIMES BOLD: Series No. 334

ABCJabcde
72 pt.

DEFG fghijkl
60 pt.

HIKLM mnopqrs
48 pt.

NOPQR tuvwxyz:;
42 pt.

STUVWX abcdefghijk
36 pt.

YZ1234567890 lmnopqrstuvwx
30 pt.

DESPITE the increased weight there is 24 pt.

LITTLE difference in width between these caps and 18 pt.

THOSE of Times Roman; in the lower case the bold is the narrower 14 pt.

12 pt. solid

but Perpetua and Gill Sans, designed by Eric Gill, are unquestionably as original as a type can be. Eric Gill has left his mark in the history of type. Nothing has been said of America so

10 pt. solid

far, because until recently America did not contribute anything of importance to type design. No outline of type history would now be complete without the name of Frederic Goudy who died in 1947, having produced over 100 different types. It is only to be expected

8 pt. solid

that a considerable proportion of such a large output should prove ephemeral, but Kennerley, Goudy Modern, do not tarnish with time. One cannot but pay tribute to this G.O.M. of type who twice in his life lost all his possessions by fire, but like the Phœnix he rose undaunted from calamity and went on to create new

6 pt. solid

letter forms. Another name from America is that of Bruce Rogers who designed Centaur on the Jenson model, and in some opinions improved on the old letter. Elegant and unquestionably beautiful, it is perhaps too light in colour for very wide employment. So far in this book we have discussed briefly general theoretical considerations of an approach to type with a few of the technical terms explained and a nomenclature given. It now remains to suggest a method of study of the type faces themselves in order to learn to

TIMES BOLD TITLING NO. 2: Series No. 328

72 pt. ABCDEFGH

60 pt. IJKLMNOPQR

48 pt. STUVWXYZ&£123

42 pt. 4567890ABCDEFGHI

36 pt. JKLMNOPQRSTUVWXY

30 pt. ABCDEFGHIJK 9

24 pt. LMNOPQRSTUVW

18 pt. XYZ&1234567890£ABCD

EFGHIJKLMNOPQRSTUV 14 p

ABCDEFGHIJKLMNOPQRSTUV 12 p

ABCDEFGHIJKLMNOPQRSTUVWXYZ5 10 p

ABCDEFGHIJKLMNOPQRSTUVWXYZ & ?!2 8 pt

TIMES BOLD TITLING: Series No. 332

48 pt. ABCDEFGHIJ

36 pt. LMNOPQ

Z&£?1234567890 24 p

30 pt. RSTUVWXY

ABCDEFGHIJK 18 p

TIMES EXTENDED TITLING: Series No. 339

ABCDEFHIJKL 48 pt.

MNOPQRSTUVW 42 pt.

XYZ?!(&)1234567890£ 36 pt.

ABCDEFGHIJKLMNOPQR 30 pt.

4 pt. STUVWXYZ&? ABCDEFGHIJKLMNOPQRS£ 12 pt.

8 pt. ABCDEFGHIJKL TUVWXYZ&£1234567890ABCDEFJ 10 pt.

4 pt. MNOPQRSTUVWXYZ£ GHIKLMNOPQRSTUVWXYZ&£12345678 8 pt.

TIMES TITLING: Series No. 329

ABCDEFGHIJKLMN 48 pt.

OPQRSTUVWXYZ(&12 42 pt.

34567890ABCDEFGHIJKLMNOPQ 30 pt.

RSTUVWXYZ&£ABCDEFGHIJKLMNOPQ 24 pt.

RSTUVWXYZ&1234567890£ABCDEFGHIJKLM 18 pt.

NOPQRSTUVWXYZ&1234567890£ABCDEFGHIJKLMNOPQR 14 pt.

Miscellaneous

UNDER this heading are included types which, for various reasons, it was not thought wise to include in the first edition of this book, but which are now likely to be of interest.

Latin, with its triangular, long pointed serifs is proving itself popular not only amongst typographers but amongst letterers and designers who make improvisations on the 'Latin' theme by compressing it, fattening it, elongating it and whatever variation the designer thinks fit. Chisel is based on Wide Latin.

'Three dimensional' or 'shaded' letters are also popular with some designers. Thorne Shaded and Figgins Shaded are two good nineteenth century revivals, but Profil is a mid twentieth century design.

Script types are here represented briefly with a typical copperplate, which, though cut recently is influenced by nineteenth century scripts. On the other hand Mistral is a freely drawn script which is undoubtedly twentieth century.

Castellar has a classical grace which endears itself to literary publishers. In contrast, Teachest is a stencil letter based on the kind of letters stencilled on packing cases, which is more likely to be used for advertising. Playbill, as the name implies, is a revival of the type that was used so often on early Victorian Playbills. Its rich colour and gay associations make it still a useful display type.

Ornamented letters, which do not really come within the scope of this book, are represented by but one, though very beautiful example Sapphire. This is designed by one of the best living letterers Herman Zapf. Sapphire is very legible despite the decoration and is a really pretty letter in the best sense of the word pretty.

FIGGINS CONDENSED No. 2 (Stevens Shanks)

A condensed fat face following the usual English design of the time and taken over from the foundry of V. and J. Figgins.

ABCDEFGHIJKLMNOPQRSTU VWXYZÆŒ 1224567890 abcdefghijklmnopqrstuvwxyz

FIGGINS SHADED (Stevens Shanks)

Three-dimensional capitals and figures with white faces. Probably designed by A. Bessemer, the letter first appeared in Bessemer and Catherwood's specimen of 1825, although Vincent Figgins has shown a 24 point of different design as early as 1815. The first specimen shown here is slightly heavier and more oblique in shading than the original 24 point.

ABCDEFGHIJKLMNOPQRSTUVW XYZŒÆ&£1234567800 ABCDEFG

FESTIVAL (Monotype)

Specially designed to commemorate the Festival of Britain and for Festival advertising by Phillip Boydell and his associates of the London Press Exchange. Based upon condensed sans italic capitals it has a three-dimensional form making it suitable for use in exhibition display typography. Capitals and numerals only.

THE QUICK LAZY FOX

LATIN BOLD CONDENSED (Stephenson Blake)

ABCDEFGHIJKLMNOPQRSTUVWXYZ
abcdefghijklmnopqrstuvwxyz

ELONGATED LATIN (Stephenson Blake)

ABCDEFGHIJKLMNOPQRSTUVWXYZ abcdefghijklmnopqrst

PLAYBILL (Stephenson Blake)

A condensed, reversed Egyptian, in which the serifs are heavier than the main strokes. It is a revival of a Victorian type. The style was at first called FRENCH ANTIQUE, or sometimes ITALIAN.

ABCDEFGHIJKLMN rstuvwxyz
OPQRSTUVWXYZ abcdefghijklmnopqrstu

TEA CHEST (Stephenson Blake)

A set of bold, condensed capitals with stubby serifs and with white gaps in some strokes, that is to say a stencil letter. The round letters have a break in the top and another at the foot.

THE BROWN FOX

THORNE SHADED (Stephenson Blake)

One of the earliest three-dimensional letters, dating from about 1820. The greatly modified design is based on the contemporary fat face capitals, but with thicker serifs.

ABCDEFGHIJKLMN1234

SAPPHIRE (Stempel)

Designed by Hermann Zapf. Decorated capitals of fat face design.

ABCDEFGHIJKLMNOPQR

WIDE LATIN (Stephenson Blake)

48 pt.

ABCDE
FGHIJK
LMONP
QRSTU
VWXYZ
abcdefgh
ijklmno
pqrstuv
wxyz£&
1234567

14 pt. ABCDEFGHIJ abcdefghijklmn

PROFIL (Haas)

Designed by Eugen and Max Lenz. A set of three-dimensional capitals and figures, which are inclined. The heavy black letters are rimmed with a white line.

ABCDEFGHIJKLM
NOPQRSTUVWXYZ
1234567890

CASTELLAR (Monotype)

Designed by John Peters. A set of shaded capitals and figures. The serifs are long and thin.

ABCDEFGHIJKL
MNOPQRSTUVX

MISTRAL (Olive 1953, Amsterdam 1955)

Designed by Roger Excoffon. An informal, true script, the forerunner of CHOC, but of lighter weight and less roughly drawn. The letters of the lower case are close-setting.

ABCDEFGHIJKLMNOPQRSTUVWXYZ
abcdefghijklmnopqrstuvwxyz 1234567

COPPERPLATE BOLD (Stephenson Blake 1953)

A bold face of the English copperplate script, similar in style, but not in weight, to MARINA.

ABCDEFGHIJKLMNO
PQRSTUVWXYZ abcdefg
hijklmnopqrstuvwxyz1234567890

This four-page inset has been set on a 'Mono-photo' machine and printed by offset lithography. Until the introduction of a filmsetting machine, when reading matter was reproduced by lithography or photogravure it had to be set in type and a sharp proof taken which was then photographed. Positives were then made and printed down on to the plate.

Movable types are no longer necessary for these processes. A film is produced in the filmsetting machine on which the reading matter appears spaced out and in correct position.

The principle on which these machines operate is similar to the principle employed in the hot metal casting machines. For casting type in hot metal each key on the keyboard releases a matrix which is positioned to receive a charge of molten metal. Each key on a filmsetting machine operates the placing of a negative of a letter of the alphabet (or other character) in position to be printed photographically in its correct order on a sheet of film. The sheet of film represents whole pages which can then be

imposed in the proper position and printed down on to the plate.

As the machine is virtually a complex photographic enlarger, one image of a character can easily be enlarged to a great number of sizes. But these are related to the traditional typographic sizes: the 'Monophoto' sets type in sizes from 6 point to 12 point in one point steps and from 12 point to 24 point at two point intervals. There is therefore a wider range of sizes than is normal with hot metal types.

It is also possible to vary the space between lines by as little as half a point. In hot metal terminology —any type size can be produced on any body in steps of half a point. Thus 10 point type can be set with lines the distance apart equivalent to being on a body of $10\frac{1}{2}$, 11, $11\frac{1}{2}$, 12, $12\frac{1}{2}$ points and so on.

Characters such as small caps, accented letters, mathematical signs, fractions etc., are available for filmsetting in every size from 6 to 24 point.

The film as it comes from the filmsetter is used not only for the production of plates for lithographic printing but for the making of line-blocks.

For lithography the positive is used in the normal way. To make a line-block a negative is employed. Powderless etching by the Dow or Dirats process has simplified and greatly accelerated the production of relief-printing plates such as line-blocks and halftones for letterpress printing.

Filmsetting has helped to improve the standard of lithographic printing of text-matter. Hitherto greyness and lack of sharpness had characterised the reproduction of type by lithography, but the filmsetter has made it possible to obtain a clear crisp image on the plate and thus give the litho-printer a better chance to produce a good impression. (He still needs an efficient press, really black ink and the right paper).

The printers of this inset claim that properly used for suitable work the filmsetting machine can produce better quality print, more quickly and at lower cost than existing methods. In certain circumstances all three of these advantages may be gained; in other conditions perhaps

only one or two of them.

While it is true that corrections of filmsetting can be made, it is a lengthy process and too many alterations at the proof stage could wipe out any economy that might otherwise be made. It is therefore important that 'copy' should be carefully prepared and no major alterations made to continuous masses of run-on copy. On the other hand, filmsetting is suitable for jobs in which the copy is broken up into individual self-contained areas which can easily be moved or re-set if alterations are considered.

There are a number of different filmsetting machines, mostly made by the manufacturers of hot metal casting machines. It will be noticed that the type-faces displayed on this and the following three pages are designs that already exist as hot metal types and have been produced by means of punch and matrix. The method of manufacture tends to influence the shape of a letter but it remains to be seen whether the photosetter will lead to the designing of letters specially adapted to that miraculous machine.

24 Baskerville

Bembo

22 ABCDEFPabcdefghijr
ABCDEGOabcdefghikno

ABCDEFGIabcdefghijkt
ABCDEFGIabcdefghijklm

20 ABCDEFJLabcdefghijkt
ABCDEFGRabcdefghijkmr

ABCDEFGILabcdefghijknz
ABCDEFGJLabcdefghijklnoq

18 ABCDEFGNabcdefghijklo
ABCDEFGIKabcdefghijklmz

ABCDEFGHTabcdefghjklnoz
ABCDEFGHKabcdefghijklmnw

16 ABCDEFGHLabcdefghijklmr
ABCDEFGHIRabcdefghijklmnov

ABCDEFGHIJTabcdefghjkloprtz
ABCDEFGHLOabcdefghijklmnopu

14 ABCDEFGHIJLabcdefghijklmnw
ABCDEFGHIJMabcdefghijklmnopqv

ABCDEFGHIJNOabcdefghijklmnrstu
ABCDEFGHIJLWabcdefghijklmnopqxz

12 ABCDEFGHIJLSZabcdefghijklmnopqt
ABCDEFGHIJKMSabcdefghijklmnopqrstw

ABCDEFGHIJKLWabcdefghjklmopqruy
ABCDEFGHIJKNUabcdefghijklmnopqruvy

11 ABCDEFGHIJKLPSabcdefghijklmnopqrw
ABCDEFGHIJKLMRabcdefghijklmnopqrstvwy

ABCDEFGHIJKLOWabcdefghijklmnopqrtw
ABCDEFGHIJKLNWabcdefghijklmnopqrstvwx

10 ABCDEFGHIJKLOPZabcdefghijklmnopqrtuw
ABCDEFGHIJKLMPWabcdefghijklmnopqrstuvwxy

ABCDEFGHIJKLMNOabcdefghijklmnopqrsuvx
ABCDEFGHIJKLMPWabcdefghijklmnopqrstuvwzr

9 ABCDEFGHIJKLMNOPabcdefghijklmnopqrstuwzr
ABCDEFGHIJKLMNOQSabcdefghijklmnopqrstuvwxyzce

ABCDEFGHIJKLMNOSTabcdefghijklmnopqrstuvxyt
ABCDEFGHIJKLMNOPVabcdefghijklmnopqrstuvwxyzk

8 ABCDEFGHIJKLMNOPQSabcdefghijklmnopqrstuvwxyzt
ABCDEFGHIJKLMNOPSTZabcdefghijklmnopqrstuvwxyzabcdg

ABCDEFGHIJKLMNOQRWabcdefghijklmnopqrstuvwxyzlr
ABCDEFGHIJKLMNOPQVYabcdefghijklmnopqrstuvwxyzabcdg

7 ABCDEFGHIJKLMNOPQWabcdefghijklmnopqrstuvwxyzrt
ABCDEFGHIJKLMNOPQWXabcdefghijklmnopqrstuvwxyzabcdez

ABCDEFGHIJKLMNOPQRTVabcdefghijklmnopqrstuvwxyzatw
ABCDEFGHIJKLMNOPQVWLabcdefghijklmnopqrstuvwxyzabcdefm

6 ABCDEFGHIJKLMNOPQRSTUZabcdefghijklmnopqrstuvwxyzabcdefz
ABCDEFGHIJKLMNOPQRSTUWJabcdefghijklmnopqrstuvwxyzabcdefghijklz

ABCDEFGHIJKLMNOPQRSTUWLabcdefghijklmnopqrstuvwxyzabcdefglz
ABCDEFGHIJKLMNOPQRSTUVWabcdefghijklmnopqrstuvwxyzabcdefghijkmq

ALL SIZES ARE AVAILABLE IN BOLD as well as in Roman and Italic. ABCDEFGHIJKLMNOPRWZ abcdefghijklmnopqrstuvwxyzabcdf

ALL SIZES ARE AVAILABLE IN BOLD as well as in Roman and Italic. ABCDEFGHIJKLMNOPQRSTVYW abcdefghijklmnopqrstuvwxyzabcdfgs

24 Gill Sans

Imprint

22 ABCDEFGabcdefghiv
ABCDEFGKabcdefghijt

ABCDIJLabcdefghir
ABCDGOabcdefghkn

20 ABCDEFGLabcdefghijkl
ABCDEFGHLabcdefghijko

ABCDEFZabcdefghmt
ABCDEHIabcdefghijkq

18 ABCDEFGIKabcdefghijklr
ABCDEFGHLSabcdefghijknr

ABCDEFGIabcdefghijlm
ABCDEFGIabcdefghijklw

16 ABCDEFGKWabcdefghijknrz
ABCDEFGHKWabcdefghijklnor

ABCDEFGIZabcdefghijklnz
ABCDEFILOabcdefghijklnpt

14 ABCDEFGHIJLTabcdefghijklmrw
ABCDEFGHIJKNRabcdefghijklmnop

ABCDEFGHIZabcdefghijklmnz
ABCDEFGHILabcdefghijklmnop

12 ABCDEFGHIJKMNabcdefghijklmnopw
ABCDEFGHIJKLMNPabcdefghijklmnoprsv

ABCDEFGHIJLPabcdefghijklmnopq
ABCDEFGHIVWabcdefghijklmnopqrs

11 ABCDEFGHIJKLOPSabcdefghijklmnopqru
ABCDEFGHIJKLMOUZabcdefghijklmnopqrstv

ABCDEFGHIJKLZabcdefghijklmnopqrv
ABCDEFGHIJKLPabcdefghijklmnopqrzm

10 ABCDEFGHIJKLMNPTabcdefghijklmnopqrsuv
ABCDEFGHIJKLMNORSTabcdefghijklmnopqrsuwx

ABCDEFGHIJKLPRabcdefghijklmnopqrstz
ABCDEFGHIJKLPSabcdefghijklmnopqrsturs

9 ABCDEFGHIJKLMNOQTabcdefghijklmnopqrstuvw
ABCDEFGHIJKLMNOPQWPabcdefghijklmnopqrstuvwyz

ABCDEFGHIJKLMNUabcdefghijklmnopqrstuwz
ABCDEFGHIJKLMNXabcdefghijklmnopqrstuvxyz

8 ABCDEFGHIJKLMNOPQRUabcdefghijklmnopqrstuvwxza
ABCDEFGHIJKLMNOPQRSTUZabcdefghijklmnopqrstuvwxyzac

ABCDEFGHIJKLMNOPQabcdefghijklmnopqrstuvwzm
ABCDEFGHIJKLMNOPTabcdefghijklmnopqrstuvwxyzst

7 ABCDEFGHIJKLMNOPQRWYabcdefghijklmnopqrstuvwxyzst
ABCDEFGHIJKLMNOPQRSTUVWabcdefghijklmnopqrstuvwxyzabct

ABCDEFGHIJKLMNOPQSPabcdefghijklmnopqrstuvwxyzbn
ABCDEFGHIJKLMNOQUWabcdefghijklmnopqrstuvwxyzabtw

6 ABCDEFGHIJKLMNOPQRSTUVZFabcdefghijklmnopqrstuvwxyzabcdfo
ABCDEFGHIJKLMNOPQRSTUVWXZHabcdefghijklmnopqrstuvwxyzabcdefmt

ABCDEFGHIJKLMNOPQRSWMabcdefghijklmnopqrstuvwxyzabcdew
ABCDEFGHIJKLMNOPQRSTZIabcdefghijklmnopqrstuvwxyzabcdefghk

ALL SIZES ARE AVAILABLE IN BOLD as well as in Roman and Italic. ABCDEFGHIJKLMNORTY abcdefghijklmnopqrstuvwxyzabim

ALL SIZES ARE AVAILABLE IN BOLD as well as in Roman and Italic. ABCDEFGHIJKLMNOPQRY abcdefghijklmnopqrstuvwxyzabdh

24 Plantin   Times

22 ABCDPWabcdefgmr
ABCDWZabcdefghkn
  ABCDEFIabcdefghkt
ABCDEGIabcdefghrw

20 ABCDMWabcdefghikr
ABCDEFLabcdefghijko
  ABCDEGVabcdefghinv
ABCDEFMabcdefghijlw

18 ABCDEFGIabcdefghijlm
ABCDEFHIabcdefghijklw
  ABCDEFLTabcdefghijklr
ABCDEFGKabcdefghijklx

16 ABCDEFIRTabcdefghijklnz
ABCDEFGJRabcdefghijklnor
  ABCDEFGHIabcdefghijklnu
ABCDEFGHLabcdefghijklmn

14 ABCDEFGILTabcdefghijklmov
ABCDEFGHIRabcdefghijklmnop
  ABCDEFGHLPabcdefghijklmstz
ABCDEFGHIJZabcdefghijklmnor

12 ABCDEFGHKLZabcdefghijklmnopq
ABCDEFGHIKMabcdefghijklmnopwy
  ABCDEFGHIJKNabcdefghijklmnopw
ABCDEFGHIJLPZabcdefghijklmnopqw

11 ABCDEFGHIJKOPabcdefghijklmnopqrv
ABCDEFGHIJLMZabcdefghijklmnopqrzm
  ABCDEFGHIJKMPabcdefghijklmnopqru
ABCDEFGHIJKLRTabcdefghijklmnopqrsw

10 ABCDEFGHIJKLPRabcdefghijklmnopqrstz
ABCDEFGHIJKLPVabcdefghijklmnopqrswzc
  ABCDEFGHIJKLPSVabcdefghijklmnopqrstw
ABCDEFGHIJKLNORabcdefghijklmnopqrsuxy

9 ABCDEFGHIJKLMNUabcdefghijklmnopqrstvwx
ABCDEFGHIJKLMOWabcdefghijklmnopqrstuvxyz
  ABCDEFGHIJKLMNOVabcdefghijklmnopqrstuvwz
ABCDEFGHIJKLMNPRSabcdefghijklmnopqrstuvwzis

8 ABCDEFGHIJKLMNOPTabcdefghijklmnopqrstuvxyzb
ABCDEFGHIJKLMNOPQabcdefghijklmnopqrstuvwxyzw
  ABCDEFGHIJKLMNOWXabcdefghijklmnopqrstuvwxyk
ABCDEFGHIJKLMNOPQXabcdefghijklmnopqrstuvwxyzst

7 ABCDEFGHIJKLMNOPWMabcdefghijklmnopqrstuvwxyzbn
ABCDEFGHIJKLMNOPRTZabcdefghijklmnopqrstuvwxyzabhz
  ABCDEFGHIJKLMNOPQUabcdefghijklmnopqrstuvwxyzg
ABCDEFGHIJKLMNOPRSVabcdefghijklmnopqrstuvwxyzalt

6 ABCDEFGHIJKLMNOPQRSUVIabcdefghijklmnopqrstuvwxyzabcdefr
ABCDEFGHIJKLMNOPQRSUEIabcdefghijk'mnopqrstuvwxyzabcdefghk
  ABCDEFGHIJKLMNOPQRSTVZabcdefghijklmnopqrstuvwxyzabcdeg
ABCDEFGHIJXLMNOPQRSTUZIabcdefghijklmnopqrstuvwxyzabcdefgr

ALL SIZES ARE AVAILABLE IN BOLD as well as in Roman and Italic. ABCDEFGHIJKLMNORTZ abcdefghijklmnopqrstuvwxyzabm

ALL SIZES ARE AVAILABLE IN BOLD as well as in Roman and Italic. ABCDEFGHIJKLMNOPQRSTUWM abcdefghijklmnopqrstuvwxyzabcdefghmr

ALBERTUS: The name of a display type.

ALDUS MANUTIUS (b. 1450, d. 1514): The great Venetian publisher and printer. Famous for *The Dream of Poliphilus*, one of the finest illustrated books ever produced. Our old-style types are descended from his roman types and he was the first to cast the sloping letter we know as italic.

ALIGN (Alignment: To arrange letters, words etc., on the same horizontal line.

AMPERSAND: The short version of 'and'—& *&*. It is a development of the scribes' Latin *et* meaning and.

ANTIQUE: The name of a type design. The name given to a wide variety of papers having a roughish surface.

ARABIC FIGURES: The figures in general use: 1234567890.

ARM: The projecting horizontal strokes on such letters as T, E.

ART PAPER: Paper coated with a composition, generally china clay, to give a smooth, glossy surface; unpleasant, but necessary for printing half-tone blocks properly.

ASCENDER: The part of a lower-case letter which projects above the mean-line, as in b, h, l, etc.

BACK (of a type: The plane opposite and parallel to that containing the nick.

BANK (paper): The name applied to a variety of thin, tough and more or less transparent papers such as is used for typewriting. Excellent for layouts, and is often used by artists for sketching from nature.

BASE LINE: The imaginary line on which the base of capital letters rest. *See page 12.*

BASKERVILLE: An excellent type named after John Baskerville of Birmingham (1706–75), writing master, manufacturer of lacquer work and finally printer and type designer. Invented hot-pressed paper.

BEARD: The space between the base line and the front of the type (stamp).

BEMBO: One of the finest book types, based on the type in a tract by Cardinal Bembo and published by Aldus in the late 15th century.

BEVEL: The sloping portion on type between the face and the shoulder.

BLACK LETTER: Type based on medieval script such as the plain man would call 'Old English'. Also called Text, or Textura.

BODONI: A typical 'Modern' Face based on the designs of Giambattista Bodoni of Parma (1740–1813).

BODY: A synonym for shank, the rectangular prism of metal from which the face of the type is raised.

BOLD: The name given to a thickened version of a type design.

BOND: Almost the same as Bank paper (q.v.) but slightly thicker. Useful for layouts.

BOWL: The rounded part of such letters as P, B and the upper part of g to distinguish it from the lower part known as the loop.

BROADSIDE: An unfolded sheet of any standard size of paper.

CALENDERED PAPER: Paper made smooth by passing it between rollers.

CALLIGRAPHY: Fine writing.

CAP-LINE: The imaginary line which runs along the top of capital letters. *See page 12.*

CASLON OLD FACE: The most venerable of old-face types, keeping alive the name of its designer, William Caslon (1692–1766), one-time engraver of gun barrels.

CENTAUR: A type by Bruce Rogers based on Jenson's fifteenth-century Venetian design.

CLARENDON: A type with heavy serifs, as this **ABCDE.** Originally designed for dictionaries.

CLUMP: Thick metal spacing material.

COATED PAPER: *See* Art Paper.

CONDENSED: Type in which the letters are narrower than normal. E.g. condensed.

COUNTER: The enclosed parts of a letter. *See p.* 12.

COUNTER-PUNCH: The punch used to strike the counters when making the master-punch which in turn makes the matrix.

CROWN: Standard size of printing paper, that is, 15″ × 20″.

CURSIVE: Literally, resembling handwriting; flowing rather than formal.

DEMY: Standard size of printing paper namely, $17\frac{1}{2}'' \times 22\frac{1}{2}''$.

DESCENDER: Those parts of such letters as g, p, q which descend below the base line.

EM: The square of the body in any size of type. As a unit of measurement the 12 pt. em (pica) is understood.

EM QUAD: A space which is the same dimension set-wise as point-wise. Known to compositors as a 'mutton'.

EN: Half an em. Said to be the average width of a letter. Also referred to as a 'nut'.

FACE (of a type): The part of a type stamp which comes into contact with the paper.

FLOWERS: Printers' ornaments.

FOLIO: The size of a sheet of paper folded in half. The numbers placed on each page of a book.

FOOT (of a type): The plane, parallel to the face, on which the body rests. (Of a page): the bottom.

FOUNT: A complete set of types comprising a proportionate number of every letter of the alphabet and other sorts as ? £ etc. Derived from the word 'fund', that is a fund of type from which letters may be drawn.

FULL POINT: Full stop.

FURNITURE: Pieces of wood or metal to space out type at the head of chapters, title-pages, margins, etc.

GARAMOND: The name applied to a popular type once thought to be designed by Claude Garamond, a sixteenth-century French type designer, now known to be by Jean Jannon.

GILL SANS: One of the finest sanserif letters, designed by Eric Gill.

GOTHIC: A loosely used term applied absurdly to sanserif types and appropriately to black letter (Old English, Textura).

GRANJON: A type by G. W. Jones based on Garamond. At present available only on the Linotype.

GROTESQUE: A name given to some sanserif types.

HAIRSPACE: A very thin space for spacing letters, p. 10.

HARD-SIZED: A term applied to paper that has been given considerable sizing.

HEAD: The top of a page.

HEIGHT TO PAPER: 0.918″.

IONIC: The name of a type, as this ABCDEFGHI

ITALIC: Type on which the letters slope up to the right. Known on the continent as Kursiv (cursive).

JENSON, NICHOLAS: Famous Venetian printer whose roman type has been the model for many type designers.

JUSTIFY: To space type in a composing stick so that the line is filled either with type characters or spaces.

KERN: That part of a type which overhangs the body.

LEAD: Thin strips of metal below type-high, used to space lines, p. 10.

LETTERSPACING: Space placed between each letter of a word.

LIGATURE: The connecting link between two letters that are joined together. Often mis-used in the sense of logotype, that is, two or more letters cast on one body.

LINOTYPE: A machine operated by a key-board for casting solid lines of type as distinct from single letters.

LOOP: The lower part of g.

LOWER-CASE: 'Small letters' (minuscules), so called because when all type was set by hand two cases were used, one being arranged on a frame higher than the other. The upper case held the capital letters, the lower case held the 'small letters'.

MAJUSCULES: Capital letters.

MANILA: Smooth, tough paper, often used for business envelopes and letter files.

MATRIX: The mould from which the face of type is cast.

MEAN-LINE: The imaginary line that runs along the top of lower-case a, n, x, etc.

MEASURE: The length of line to which type is set.

MEDIUM: A standard size of paper, 18″ × 23″.

MIDDLE SPACE: A small piece of metal for spacing words. There are four to an em.

MINUSCULE: 'Small letter' or lower case.

MODERN FACE: The kind of type in which the point of maximum stress is central; serifs of lower-case l, h, b, d, n are at right angles. *See p.* 19.

'MONOTYPE': A machine comprising a separate keyboard and caster for casting types singly but in the sequence of the manuscript.

MOULD: The name applied to the mould in which the body or shank of a type is cast, to distinguish it from the mould which casts the letter, which is known as the Matrix (q.v.).

MOXON: The author of the first account in English describing the craft of typefounding and printing. It appears in *Mechanic Exercises*, published in 1683.

MUTTON: Printers slang for an em.

NICK: The slot on the body of the type to assist the compositor in getting all letters in his composing stick the right way round. Nicks are placed uppermost in the stick.

NONPAREIL: The name of an old type-size about 6 points. Pronounced 'Nonprul'.

NUT: Printers slang for an en.

OCTAVO: The size resulting from folding a sheet into eight leaves.

OLD-FACE TYPE: The name given to an important group of types. The chief characteristics being:
(1) point of maximum stress at an angle;
(2) serifs of lower-case h, l, m, etc., at an angle;
(3) gradual transition from thick to thin strokes in the curved letters. *See p.* 19.

PERIOD: A full point (full stop).

PICA: The name of an old type-size approximately 1/6″ or 12 points. Many use the term as being more desirable than the term 'em' as the unit of measurement.

PIE: Type that has been spilled chaotically and mixed.

PLANTIN: A type face named after the famous Antwerp printer, Christopher Plantin. The 'MONOTYPE' Plantin (110) is quite different from founders' Plantin.

POINT SYSTEM: The system by which all typographic material is manufactured to sizes which are exact multiples of a point. The English and American point is 0.0138″, or more accurately 72 points = 0.9966″. The Didot point used on the Continent is slightly larger.

POINT OF MAXIMUM STRESS: The thickest part of curved letters, like O, e, etc. *See p.* 12.

PUNCH: A piece of steel with a letter engraved on the end, which is struck into another piece of metal to form the matrix from which type is cast.

QUAD: Quadrats—pieces of metal below type-high used for spacing; the usual sizes are: en, em, 2, 3, and 4 ems.

QUARTO: The size arrived at by folding a sheet into four.

RECTO: The right-hand page of an open book.

REGLET: Thin strips of wood for spacing lines of types.

ROMAN: The name often applied to the Latin alphabet which is used in most European and American languages. It is also used in the sense of upright letters (roman) as distinguished from sloping (italic).

ROMAN NUMERALS: I = 1, II = 2, III = 3, IV = 4, V = 5, VI = 6, VII = 7, VIII = 8, IX = 9, X = 10, L = 50, C = 100, M = 1,000, XL = 40, LX = 60, D = 500, MCMXLVIII = 1948. MCMLXI = 1961.

ROYAL: A standard size of paper, 20″ × 25″.

RULE: Strips of metal with a type-high face that print as lines, thus ————————————.

SANSERIF: Letters without serifs.

SMALL CAPS: Letters, like capitals in shape, but ranging with the base line and mean-line of the lower-case letters in the size cast. Usually only cast in sizes 14 pt. and smaller. Useful in catalogues of books, etc.

SCRIPT TYPE: Type that imitates handwriting; though it may resemble 'copperplate' it may appear to be written with a brush.

SERIFS: The projecting finishing strokes at the stems of letters.

SET: The width of a type character. *See p.* 7.

SHANK: *See* Body.

SHOULDER: The flat top of the body from which the bevel slopes up to the face.

SLUG: The name given to the line of type cast in one piece as on a Linotype.

SOLID: Lines of type with no leads between are said to be 'set solid'.

SORTS: Individual types as distinct from a complete fount.

SPACES: Pieces of metal, below type-height, for spacing letters and words.

SWASH LETTERS: Flourished italic letters as *ADNPT*

THICK SPACE: A space of which there are three to an em. *See p.* 10.

THIN SPACE: A space of which there are five to an em. *See p.* 10.

TITLING: Capital letters cast 'full face' on the body. Hence there is no beard on titling and no lower-case to match.

TYPOGRAPHER: Roughly what an architect is to building. That is, a person responsible for the appearance and character of printed matter and who therefore must be knowledgeable in all the processes of printing, paper, binding, etc., while possessing the good taste to use the materials effectively.

UPPER CASE: Capital letters—from the fact that caps used to be kept in the upper of a pair of cases, the lower of which held the small letters (lower case). The sentence may be heard 'set that in upper and lower', meaning 'Set that in capitals and small letters'.

VERSO: The left-hand page of an open book.

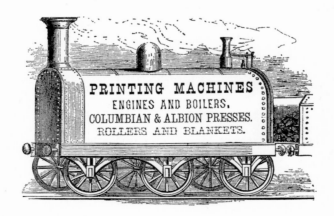